THE
AMERICAN
PUBLISHER

THE AMERICAN PUBLISHER

Paying the Cost of Corporatism and Censorship
for Writing the Truth about Cuba, Russia,
and the War on Terror

JAY FRASER

Affiliated Writers of America
Casa Grande, Arizona

Published by Affiliated Writers of America
An Imprint of Alexander & Hayes Publishing, Inc.
P.O. Box 11107
Casa Grande, Arizona 85130
520-709-6658

Cover Art, Cover Illustration(s), and Cover Design Copyright 2010 by Alexander & Hayes Publishing, Inc.
Book Design, Typesetting, and Computer Graphics by Jayme Fraser

Library of Congress Cataloging-in-Publication Data
Fraser, Jay.
The American publisher : paying the cost of corporatism and censorship for writing the truth about Cuba, Russia, and the War on Terror / Jay Fraser.
p. cm.
Includes index.
ISBN 978-1-879915-22-0 (alk. paper)
1. Fraser, Jay. 2. Publishers and publishing--United States--Biography. 3. Book industries and trade--Political aspects--United States. 4. Moore, Robin, 1925-2008. Moscow connection. 5. Censorship--United States. 6. Business and politics--United States. 7. Mass media--Objectivity--United States. I. Title.
Z473.F73F73 2010
070.5092--dc22
[B]
2010014056

To the guard who took me into the room where
Hemingway wrote in Havana, whose spirit and courage
I will never forget, and to all of the people in the world who
have had the courage to write the truth.

CONTENTS

PART TWO

Acknowledgments

Thanks to Jim Milliot, for his dedication to this industry, to the noble enterprise of writing and publishing, and for helping me discover truth. Without that moment of truth in his office, part of my quest may not ever have been discovered. He has taught me many things, some of which are aspects of this industry which are hard to understand, and sometimes, even harder to accept. Every publisher in this country who reads his writing has benefited in some way from his knowledge and personal sacrifices to deliver it.

Thanks to my daughter, Jayme Fraser, for encouraging me to finish this book after hearing or seeing parts of this story as she grew up. She always showed her respect for me as a publisher and a father even during the hardest times in my life. And, thanks to her, not only for choosing a career in journalism where she has acquired the skills to help edit, typeset, and package this book, but for choosing to do so.

Thanks to Colonel Robert Morris, US Army, for his friendship, loyalty, encouragement, and knowledge. He has contributed many ideas to the shaping of this book. He is a great man who has not only helped me finish this project, but has helped the nation through his unwavering service in the Army, and has helped countless people all over the world through his charitable organization—Partners International.

Thanks to Robin Moore, and in memory of Robin Moore, who passed away last year (bless his soul), who lived much of this story alongside me, and was the greatest writer I ever had the honor to publish. He was my strongest mentor in publishing. He taught me New York City. He taught me many things about writing, books, and the world. He endured the events in this story with honor and courage. Even during our darkest hours, he showed respect and resilience, never wavering from his duty to me as an author to the publisher. He is alive in this book. And it is with honor and pride that I tell a story that is also about Robin and our incredible times together—great author, great man, and great friend. He lives forever through his writing and in the hearts of those who read his books.

Thanks to Jack Wainwright, who taught me Washington DC, who was a good friend, who had my authors and me as guests in his home, picked me up from the airport, who hosted wonderful dinners with exciting guests, and accommodated me or all of us while we were in the District. Thanks also to Kitty Wainwright. All of this help, encouragement, knowledge, and friendship made a difference in my career as a publisher and in my understanding of Washington politics.

Thanks to Peter Grinenko for his help in my understanding of the Russian people, the Russian mafia, nuclear weapons issues, and the former Soviet Union.

Thanks to Ron Clark and Ben Franklin Press, Bertlesmann, Berryville Graphics, RR Donnelley, Walsworth Publishing, and the many other printers and tradesmen who have helped me bring my books to market in printed form.

Thanks to Dave Barbour and Curtis Brown for representing foreign rights and bringing the contracts presented in this book.

Thanks to Christopher Harper (ABC), Gary Scurka (CBS), Rebecca Sinkler (*The New York Times Book Review*), Charles Hanley (*Associated Press*), Jim Bohannon (*The Jim Bohannon Show*), Larry King (then *The Larry King Live* radio show), Debbie Sontag (*Miami Herald Book Review*), and Cindy Adams (*New York Post*).

Thanks to Western Writers of America for the Medicine Pipe Award for *People of the Whistling Waters.*

Thanks to *The New York Times Book Review, The Wall Street Journal., LA Times Book Review, Miami Herald, Boston Herald, Rocky Mountain News, Publishers Weekly, Library Journal, Booklist, Christian Science Monitor,* CBS, NPR, *Casper Star-Tribune, Wichita Eagle,* and *The Associated Press.*

Thanks to all of the other journalists, writers, magazines, newspapers, radio networks, television networks, producers, and media celebrities who have either reviewed my books, interviewed the authors I have published, given me or my authors awards, or produced stories about anything pertaining to my books or publishing endeavors. Special thanks to all of these people or entities who appear in this book. You have helped to enrich the careers of my authors and of myself. You have honored us with recognition for our work in this industry. On behalf of myself, and anyone else associated with me, who has been graced by your stories, thank you. You are too numerous to name here, but know that you are appreciated, each and every one of you.

PREFACE

I run the risk of falling victim to Robin Moore's axiom and warning. I can still hear his voice as he said it: "Jay, the one thing they'll never forgive you for is writing the truth." But I had to tell this story. Like the character in the short story who yelled into the hollow log because the knowledge ate away at him, "The king eats chaff," this story of a significant portion of my life has been eating away at me for fifteen years. I've been writing it for fifteen years. I've been yelling into hollow logs. I've been telling bits and pieces to friends, acquaintances, colleagues, and news contacts. Now, I set myself free and hope that the hollow log I shouted into has been made into paper, and like the drums in that story, will sing out my words to the world. There is a saying that the truth will set you free. I have a saying: Writing the truth will set you free.

This is a true story and a work of non-fiction. However, some people who appear in this book have not been referred to by name. In some cases, they are sources for journalists, and I have kept the names out of this book to protect their sources from being identified, and to protect the sources from being judged as the result of any impression of them presented in this book. Their names will remain the private information of the journalists who worked on their stories. In some cases, I have created a fictitious name representing the real person, such as Miss Hanson, in which case I do not know the real name. In some such cases, I wish I did. In the case where I have created a fictitious name, it is stated in the story.

I teach writing and book publishing at Central Arizona College. I teach my students to write close to their hearts, and that as they write the specific actions which caused the emotions, they will not only write powerfully, they will relive the experiences as they write about them. This book *is* my heart. I have relived it many times. Now I'm done. Even though this is not a work of fiction, I have tried assiduously, as Balzac declared a duty of every writer, to do justice to every party. But most likely, I still don't know who they all are.

FOREWORD

This book is not intended as an indictment of American journalists, publishers, distributors, or news networks. It is, rather, a cautionary tale, a call to the American public and to American journalists to demand free speech in America and nothing less—to demand real news above entertainment—to take the personal risk to demand it—and in the case of journalists and the book publishing industry—to take the personal risk to deliver it.

I was shocked when certain members of the Association of American Publishers refused to even look at censorship in America, yet rallied so hard against censorship in other countries.

American foreign policy is more important than ever now that we are in the age of terrorism and the advent of the US-based "oil-industrial complex." The US Government and oil-industrial complex to some great degree caused this terrorism movement, and continue to feed it—by refusing to hear the voices of so many who are oppressed throughout the world—by basing policy on religion and belief—by invading other nations against international law—by mistreating prisoners of war—and by mistreating its own citizens, taking away their freedom of speech, their right to privacy, their right to travel unrestricted and unmonitored—and by taking their right to even read a certain book without the government knowing exactly what they are reading at the library or buying from Amazon.com. When Carlyle Partners LP, a huge partnership owning numerous large defense contracting companies, bought the largest exporter of United States books to the rest of the world, nobody even noticed, wondered why, or even paid attention, except for Jim Milliot, of *Publishers Weekly*, and eventually, me.

PART ONE

INTRODUCTION
Rite of Passage

It was March of 1990, and finishing my Masters of Fine Arts in Creative Writing from Arizona State University in 1988, I had moved to the tiny town of Encampment, Wyoming. A blizzard was raging and I blasted through the drifts in my four-wheel-drive 1971 Chevy Blazer as I drove several blocks from my home to visit with my landlord.

We sat in her living room drinking coffee and watching the snow whip around the home, listening to the wind. It must have been three o'clock in the afternoon.

She locked eyes with me and said, "I know you're teaching English part time for the college, and I know you're writing for the newspapers, and doing your research on the West, and you've got your grant and all this, but what do you really want to do? This can't be enough for you."

"I know," I replied softly, almost inaudibly, and looked away, at the floor. It wasn't enough, and she was right. Then I looked back up at her and said, "You know what I really want to do? I want to find a good manuscript to publish. My research is not finished, and not ready to publish, and I don't know if I want to publish it myself anyway. But I've got a publishing company, you know, the one I started with my book about The Lost Dutchman Mine, and what I really want to do is build that company into a major publishing house. I need to find a good manuscript."

She sat there for a moment or two, thinking, and then she said, "I know a man who sold his ranch in Wyoming in 1955, married a Belgian Countess, and bought a ranch in Cuba. He became a CIA agent or something and got himself arrested for spying in Cuba. He spent fourteen years in prison over there. He got out ten years ago and wrote a book. But nobody will publish it. He says the government is keeping it from being published, somehow."

She definitely had my attention. "Where is he now?"

"He lives half the year in Belgium on the Royal Estate, and half the year in Tucson. It's still winter, so he's probably in Tucson."

"Do you have his phone number?"

"Yes, I think so," she said, and went into another room to get it.

When she came back with the number she gave it to me and said, "His name is Larry Lunt."

I was so poor that I didn't even have a telephone at home, and asked if I could call him right then from her phone. She nodded, and I called.

He sent me the manuscript and I loved it. It needed a lot of editing, but I thought it was a great story.

He eventually signed the book with me, and when we met in Tucson, he showed me a handwritten letter to him from Jacqueline Kennedy Onassis, on Doubleday stationary, promising Larry that she would get his book published through Doubleday. But, Larry said a week later the book got turned down. He told me this had been going on for ten years, and that he was sure the government was stopping the book.

"They're not going to stop it now," I assured him. Of course, at that point in time I had no idea just how far they would go, or how clever they could get, to interfere with production and sales of a book in America. I got a phone and a fax machine and signed a contract with the printer. I was in business with what I thought was a terrific story of sacrifice and humility and human spirit.

Because he was in the book, I wound up getting to know the CIA lawyer who represented Larry for many years in Cuban court and who lobbied for his release here in the States. In one of our first conversations, he alluded to the possibility that the Agency might not want the book out in America.

"They'll have to kill me," I replied. "I just spent six years in graduate school in English, I'm a journalist and publisher, and I'll fight to the death for free speech, especially for one of my authors."

As I said this, the words did not ring hollow. I meant every word of it. My undergraduate degree was in political science and one of my strongest beliefs was in free speech. I knew that a real democracy could not exist without it, and Lunt's story was not about child pornography; it was about politics and people's lives and the human spirit. I went on.

"Larry served his country as an agent, rightly or wrongly in Cuba, but nonetheless, he served his country, and paid a price of fourteen years in prison. He deserves the right to tell his story, and I deserve the right to publish it. This is America. We have free speech. And if we don't, I guess I'm going to find out."

The first thing that went wrong was the bank. Suddenly, and for no apparent reason, the bank seized my assets and cash flow from the wholesaler where my Dutchman Mine books were warehoused and distributed in Tucson, and, where, ultimately, the book on Cuba would be warehoused and distributed.

Out of the blue, I got a call one morning from Sterling Mahan, general manager of Treasure Chest Publications in Tucson. "Jay, do you want me to sign this letter from the bank?"

"What letter?" I asked.

"The letter from your bank ordering me to send all your checks to them instead of you. Do you want me to sign it?"

"I don't know what you're talking about," I said, dazed.

"Are you in default on a loan, or in receivership, or a lawsuit or something?" he asked.

"No! I have no idea what's going on. I have a corporate line of credit at the bank, but I haven't used any of that money yet, so I don't even owe the bank a dime."

"Well, something's going on."

"Will you fax me that letter?"

When I saw the letter, it was indeed the bank seizing my cash flow and control of the assets at the wholesaler's warehouse in Tucson. I phoned the president of Rawlins National Bank, somewhat of a friend with whom I had planned to hunt elk in the fall.

"Tom, what's the deal with this letter you sent to my wholesaler?"

"That's the way we're going to handle your account." He was short and gruff and I knew right then by the tone of his voice that something had *changed* at the bank.

"That's not the way you're going to handle it," I responded in similar tone. "Read the loan agreement. You have no authority to seize assets or cash flow unless I'm in default on the loan, *and I don't even owe the bank any money yet.*"

"That's the way we're going to handle your account."

"No it isn't. And you need to send a letter of apology to Sterling Mahan, *today.*"

"I'm not sending him a letter of apology. You'll sue me."

"I'll sue you if you don't."

They never did apologize, and it was a lock. I couldn't dare give them complete control of the cash flow and assets of my corporation, so I never used the line of credit. I had $16.74 in my corporate checking account, just sixteen dollars.

I called the printer, Ron Clark at Ben Franklin Press in Tempe, Arizona, where we were already in production. I had already printed two print runs with him on the Dutchman book, so we knew each other well.

"Ron," I said, "Something squirrelly has happened at the bank and I'm afraid to use my line of credit. What this means is, I don't know that I can pay you in thirty days."

"Well, when can you pay me?"

"I don't know, without that line of credit. But I'll tell you this. If you print the book, if I have to sell it out of the back of my car, I'll pay you as I sell them."

He said, "Jay, my janitors are stealing signatures off the pallets at night and reading this book instead of sweeping the floor. Everybody in my company loves the book. We have to print some crappy books here, you know, but this is a good book. And we're going to print it. So pay me when you can. And by the way, I don't like the way my bank treats me sometimes either."

Nobody could get to Ron Clark, but when we shipped the signatures to Roswell Binding in Phoenix, they sat on them and would not bind the book. It will be months, I was told. I stood in front of the pallets of page signatures for *Leave Me My Spirit* and presented the letter of commitment to bind the book to Mike Roswell, the president of the company, who had signed the letter himself, and begged him to bind the book and honor his own letter. He refused, saying he'd do it when he got to it; it could be months. They were very busy.

I got on the phone and found a Mormon bindery in Salt Lake City, got Yellow Freight to pick up the signatures and take them to the factory, and drove them there myself that night. The next day I was standing in front of the pallets of signatures once again, and the president of that bindery said, "We'll get on it right away."

That's what it took to get that book out. I made that sixteen dollars last for months and cut firewood that summer to support my family until the book came out. When the book was reviewed in *The New York Times* and *The Miami Herald*, I felt very proud. What I didn't know was that in distribution, I was being cheated, the bookstores were being cheated, the libraries were being cheated, and book sales were only a fraction of what they could have been. But Larry got to tell his story to the world, and I got a start building a publishing house. And now, after twenty years publishing books, I have a story to tell.

CHAPTER ONE
A Flight East

It was August 1994 and the most exciting day of my career. I had recently signed—and just finished editing in a record ten days flat—a new book about Russia which we were certain would shock the world.

I sat in the Denver airport and gazed at the other travelers seated near the gate, some dressed in fine-tailored suits with red ties, some in ill-fitting suits with dull-colored ties as if they hated wearing them, some dressed in casual shorts and T-shirts as if on a leisurely stroll in the park, some reading as if they were bored. I lived in a small town of four hundred in Wyoming, called Encampment. I was a book publisher with a few good titles, book reviews in *The New York Times*, *The Wall Street Journal*, and many, many other newspapers and magazines. Lots of acclaim, hardly any money, yet I had opened a small office on Fifth Avenue in New York and was commuting to New York from Wyoming every other week. Publishing happens in New York and I was going for it. On the West, I was an award-winning publisher of a novel on the Crow Indians in the 1800s, I published the only Native-American authored book about the Little Bighorn battle with Custer, and had several other history books about the American West. On international topics, I had a novel on African revolution and an autobiography on Cuba—the story of the CIA agent who was there during the Cuban Missile Crisis. Now I had the new book about Russia.

The day before, the man who was representative of a fictional Russian mafia character in the book, nicknamed "The Jap," had been arrested in New York City, although all of the news media in New York (which is all of the USA) was trying to downplay and outright distort the Russian mafia's activities and even existence. So I was watching to see if this would make the national news or *The New York Times*.

I surmised the seats at the gate and the other travelers again, and chose one next to a woman reading *The New York Times*. It hit me like a slap in the face. I hadn't read it yet and felt guilty that I hadn't. I couldn't get it in Encampment until two days later, and by then it was old news. The only thing I could get same-day there was the *Journal*. It was such a contrast in life, to live in the mountains of Wyoming and work in New York. When I was in New York, I read *The New York Times*, *The Wall Street Journal.*, *The Washington Post*, *The Washington Times*, *The New York Post*, and *The Boston Herald* every day. I instantly wished I would have bought a copy of at least the *Times* at the newsstand to read on the plane and see if there was a story on the Jap. It seemed like it always took a few hours, or a day, to get my fast-track mind in gear for New York.

She was reading the third page and had the paper open so the front page faced me, and as I glanced at it a small headline struck me into complete shock: "Three Russian couriers arrested in Frankfurt with plutonium."

"Ma'am!"

I had practically shouted it, and she slowly moved the paper to regard my image staring at her, somewhat aghast, but I was safe enough looking; I was wearing a black suit and a red tie like so many executives en route to New York. She guessed about me and I guessed her to be from Denver but one who prided herself on her knowledge of New York, and the world for that matter.

"May I read the front page? It's very important."

"Why, yes, of course," she said very politely, and however strong her sense of reservation and caution, a stronger sense told her it was, indeed, important, if not urgent. Common courtesy ruled, and I detected a sudden sense of intrigue beginning to build in her as she watched me read the Frankfurt story with intense excitement. I quickly jumped to the back page where the article continued, and suddenly I let out a whoop, and said, as if talking to myself, but also to her, to the world, "I knew it! I knew it! I knew it would happen!"

"You knew what?" she demanded, beginning to get irritated at her unsatiated suspense.

"I knew the Russian mafia was smuggling plutonium out of Russia and selling it to terrorists two years ago, and I'm on my way to New York with the advance copies of the first book about it! They wouldn't believe me last month—now it's front-page news. Here. Look at this while I run to the phone." I pulled a copy of the bound galleys for *The Moscow Connection* from my briefcase and handed it to her as I shot across the gate area to the telephone. The lady with the newspaper began reading the blurbs printed on the galleys and comparing them with the news of the day.

I checked in at my office and shared the breaking news in the *Times*. I was also informed that Peter Grinenko, a cop, had called from New York and said he was going to meet me at the airport. The information had been relayed with some concern, but I laughed and said it was all right. I knew who he was and it was good news. Peter was the cop who Robin Moore had fashioned the main character after in the new book about Russia. I was very excited about meeting him.

I sat down again, retrieved my galleys from the kind lady with the newspaper, and in the exhilaration of the moment settled into deep thought. It was just a moment of calm. My eye was drawn out the large windows where, although it was sunny and clear above, large, dark clouds loomed on the horizon and in the near distance above the foothills of the Rocky Mountains. My eyes seemed to go to the clouds, and the images mixed with a strange feeling which I couldn't explain. I guess I was wondering how this new arrest in Frankfurt was going to be handled in the news, and how it would all shake down in the coming weeks. Even when the real story is written, as in my case, the book sits in limbo while the publication process carries it to the media and book distribution companies. Timing is everything. Speed is everything in news. After all, it was the television which brought down the Soviet Union. That and a few brave leaders. And what gets on the television and how it does is the most politically powerful information in the world. Overnight, the television can transform fondness into hatred, allies into enemies, celebrities into someone despicable. My new book stood out in stark contrast to the fluff in the news about Russia.

So would there be efforts to stop this book? And if so, how would they do it?

In this sudden feeling of suspicion and vulnerability, I asked myself if I was just being paranoid, or if I should be concerned. I knew I should be concerned after Larry Lunt's book on Cuba. It made me even wonder about my flight. So I approached the United clerk at the gate and asked, "Is everything all right with the plane, everything on schedule?"

"Everything's fine," she said, although I noticed something different about the staff and their demeanor. Was it my imagination? Or was I being super perceptive, on the watch for a dirty trick or some unpredictable event which could disrupt my perfect timing? I somehow sensed that something was about to happen, and I went with my perceptions, my gut feelings, and my faith in my own self. I felt like a soldier in a building who senses something wrong and runs out of the building and looks back, only to see it explode behind him and totally destroyed.

My senses and intuition continued to heighten as I thought about the top news of the day, and my obvious, powerful position with this book—and what it could do, not just in sales, but to bring out a repressed view of the new Russia. Americans had no idea. It was absolutely imperative that I reach New York as scheduled. I couldn't let a canceled flight get in the way. Again, I noticed something unusual; several United clerks were now at the gate, bustling about something. I looked outside at the plane and it was a DC10, not a Boeing plane. Again the clouds caught my eye.

Something's wrong, I said to myself and looked across the terminal at the other gates, and there, just across from where I stood and only two gates down, was another flight to LaGuardia—departing only forty minutes later than my scheduled flight. I made a mental note of this and almost ran over there and switched flights, but that seemed like too much. That seemed paranoid.

Just then it was announced that the DC10 was boarding, and I went with the announcement and boarded the aircraft. I took my seat next to a middle-aged woman whose appearance suggested India, and I spoke briefly with her and learned that she was en route to New Delhi—connecting to her international flight in New York. She seemed nice enough and we chatted a bit. I had flown over New Delhi but hadn't been there. Soon, what seemed like a hundred passengers paraded past me to their seats, carrying tons of baggage and scraping seats and elbows as they streamed along through the stuffy air.

Everyone seated, the plane just sat there. Just sat there. And just sat there. *Something's wrong*, I thought again. I could feel it. And then the announcement came from the pilot: "We have a mechanical problem. There's a faulty fuel pump and we have one on the way from Seattle and it should be here when that plane arrives in—"

I knew I had to get off that plane and right at that exact moment, while the door to the gate was still open and the ramp still connected. I was already out of my seat as I thought this, and as I reached for my briefcase in the overhead compartment I said quickly and not too discretely to the woman seated next to me, "If you want to make your international flight, follow me now."

She hesitated, bewildered, and then the flight attendant rushed me from the front door of the plane and stood in my way. "You must remain seated!"

"I'm getting off this plane, ma'am. Right now."

"You can't do that! Get back in your seat!" she barked.

"No! This plane's never going to take off and you lied to us. I'm out of here!"

"You can't—"

"What are you going to do? Kidnap me?" There was room to go around her, so I turned my shoulders sideways and brushed past her in one quick move.

"—do that," she finished flatly because I was off the plane in one second flat. I felt blessed that I was able to get off without any more confrontation than that. I had no time to explain to her how important the timing of this trip to New York was for my career. What really annoyed me was that they knew about this mechanical problem—they knew this plane wasn't going to take off—and they lied to all the passengers and boarded us anyway. I'd seen it before, many times, so I knew what I had to do.

I ran and rushed to the gate for the other flight to New York, which I had noticed earlier. "Got any seats?" I asked apprehensively.

"Let me see. We have five in coach and one in first class."

"Good. Here's my ticket. Switch me to this flight. That other plane's never going to take off, and I have to be in New York today."

"I understand, sir. You're confirmed. Here's your boarding pass."

"Thank you," I said, relieved.

I found a place to sit near the gate and leaned back in my seat, calmly watching as ten minutes went by, and then the rush began as a mass exodus occurred from the DC10. Hundreds of people streamed off the plane and fought for positioning at that gate, and perhaps a hundred were astute enough to see the word LaGuardia above my gate and they stormed my gate as fast as they could run. The first few there got a seat. Then the lady from India, dazed and confused, wandered over and looked at me, hopelessly. She came over to me where I sat.

"I didn't know what to do. It was all so sudden, you getting up and leaving like that. The flight attendant said no, and I am from another country, you know."

"I know. I'm sorry. I tried to help you. Another moment and there would have been three of them blocking my way and I wouldn't have gotten off myself. You see, I've flown United all over the world, for years. And I know how they can be." I wanted to say more, for all the stress they've caused me through the years, all the canceled flights, all the lies, and all the nights I had to spend stranded somewhere, helpless, but I restrained myself. After all, she was from another country.

I had learned in my career to be alert for sudden events around me which delayed or distracted me from my daily business, especially travel. Has United always told me the truth about flights? No. I had learned to watch them, too, but not well enough.

CHAPTER TWO
The Russian-American: Act One

New York City was beautiful to me. It held the highest energy and challenge of writing and publishing, and my senses heightened as the plane approached the runway. On this particular day, I felt very fortunate that I even made it there. Although my small publishing house was located in Wyoming, I had quickly learned that to become a top publisher meant learning New York City and having an ongoing presence there. I credit Robin Moore for teaching me this and helping me to learn the city and its ways. I had debated moving to New York many times, but it would have been difficult and too expensive. So I commuted.

As soon as my feet hit the floor of the airport I was on my way to The Red Carpet Club. It was posh, and I was greeted politely at the desk. The clerk, upon seeing the name on my membership, flicked her eyes up and to the right. Before she could speak I looked over and said to the man in the corner, "You must be Peter."

"That I am."

He was built like a bulldog. His eyes were quick and he had a big smile which filled his large jaw and brought his fine facial features together nicely. He had brown eyes, brown hair, and hands which matched his thick chest and burly arms.

"Nice to meet you," I said, pleased with his warm demeanor and style. "Thanks for coming out."

"My pleasure," he responded in his smooth way.

"Let's get a table," I suggested. "Wine?"

"Vodka. Vodka martini."

I should have known, I thought as we seated ourselves. After all, he was genetically Russian and spent nearly half his time in Russia, Lithuania, Latvia, and Ukraine. He was as much like them as any New York American could be. He was taking me in as we sat there, and his quick eyes must have noticed that my wool suit was not among the best, or the best fitting, either. I still had a lot to learn about New York and sartorial taste, but I wore even a bad suit fairly well and was comfortable wearing them, which I'm sure he also noticed.

Since Robin had written so much detail about Peter in the book, I already knew a good deal about him. A Special Investigator for the Brooklyn DA's Office, Peter Grinenko spoke flawless, native Russian thanks to his mother who had moved to New York. She had lived in Kiev and grew up in Ukraine. Between the forced famine and the constant hunting of suspected Czarists by Stalin, she fled to Germany. His father had been captured by the Germans during the war, as were many Russians and Ukrainians. Because his parents were not Jewish, they were allowed to work. Peter was born near the end of the war and his parents vowed never to go back to Russia while Stalin was dictator. But he lost his father shortly after World War II. Roosevelt made an agreement with Stalin at Yalta to send all Soviet citizens back, whether they wished to return or not. His father hid out in Germany for a few years after the war, but the Americans finally found him and turned him over to the Russians. They never heard from him again. It was a bitter memory for him, and a large number of Russians had met the same fate as his father at the end of the War. His mother, grandmother, and aunt had been allowed to immigrate to America, and so they came to New York. Peter grew up in Brooklyn. Most Americans knew little or nothing about that tragic fate of so many Soviet men.

Peter had been the interpreter for the Moscow Militsia (City Police) when their boxing team had come to New York to box the NYPD Team in 1991. The visiting Chief of Militsia had asked Peter, "Where can we find this writer, this Robin Moore, who wrote *The French Connection*? Can you find him for us? We want to invite him to Moscow to write a story about our cops. About us."

Because of *Glasnost*, *The French Connection* had been translated into Russian and Gorbachev allowed it to be sold throughout Russia. The Moscow police had read it and fallen in love with Popeye Doyle, and through the movie, with Gene Hackman. They were very excited about contacting him and Peter made the arrangements.

And so the making of the novel—which I was about to publish—began. Peter came to know Robin and vice versa. Robin quickly realized that Peter represented the perfect American to be the main character in the novel: a Russian-speaking New York cop investigating the Russian mafia crime in New York and Moscow.

"You fit Robin's description of you in the book," I said.

"Oh, I do, do I?"

"Did Robin send you the page proofs?"

"Yes."

"Did you read them?"

"Yes."

"How do you like the story?"

"Interesting."

"Is it accurate?"

"Yes. It's very good."

"What about the nuclear materials? I presume you read the *Times* today."

"Of course plutonium's for sale. Everything's for sale on the black market in Russia. And the mafia is in everything. I was in the cigarette business and had to close it because I couldn't keep people from stealing—especially my employees. When a carton equals a month's wages, how could they help it? It was a game. Catch them, and call them down on it, and they respect you and stop. Maybe. Don't catch them and they don't respect you and they steal more and more.

"So if you think I had a problem with cigarettes, think what the plutonium can bring on the black market."

"I can imagine. It's pretty frightening. Of course, the book describes it."

Peter was very direct and looked me straight in the eyes as he spoke. His bold sincerity was very convincing, and his cynicism struck a strong positive note with me. The news about Russia seemed like so much bullshit—and so fake—that my shit detector was going off hourly with everything on television and in the newspapers—except for the *Times* today and that earth-shattering story about weapons-grade plutonium for sale in Frankfurt. What Peter was saying fit with what Robin had said as we edited the story.

"Robin told me it was the hardest novel he's ever written," I said. "And when I read the manuscript it was very rough, and even so, I asked him, 'Who are these people in this novel? I've never known anyone like this,' and he replied, 'Neither have I; they are Russians; and the Russian character is hard to understand. They're not like Americans.'"

"They're absolutely not like Americans. You've got to learn how the Russian mind works. Russians never say what they mean, and they are never thinking what you Americans think they are thinking. They are so fast in their minds that they are several sentences ahead of the conversation—always thinking, always deciding what they will say, and why, well in advance, and determining how much the person they are speaking with really knows, and therefore, how they can get over on them. It's all a game. Robin got it pretty close."

"You know, it irks me that literally all the press in America, and literally all the publishers—are printing the party line—that Russians are just like us and we need to invest over there and that the cold war is over—"

"Americans have no clue about Russian character."

"We've got to get this book into the news. You could help. Can I give your name and phone number to CBS and ABC? I'm meeting their producers in the morning."

"Of course."

"Will you talk with them?"

"Anything I can do to help."

"Things are hopping," I said enthusiastically, "Last week I was here in New York and nobody believed, or wanted to believe, about nuclear smuggling from Russia. Now it's front-page news."

When we walked out of The Red Carpet Club we walked down a hall and the same feeling of strangeness came over me that I had experienced aboard the plane. I regarded Peter curiously for a moment, wondering, letting my mind sift the feeling, and Peter seemed ready to spring off somewhere in a New York second with some quick goodbye.

As we left the airport, he did just that. Taking separate cabs, we parted, Peter saying, "I'm going to Brooklyn." I went straight to The Metropolitan Club at Sixtieth and Fifth Avenue where I checked into my room and got ready for the next day.

CHAPTER THREE
Red Sky at Morning, Sailor's Warning

The Metropolitan Club is one of the oldest clubs in New York City, across from the Plaza Hotel and adjacent to Central Park. Just down 60ᵗʰ Street was the Copacabana, long since closed, but the site of the famed bar scene in *The French Connection* with Gene Hackman. Anyone who doesn't know the name of the place may have seen the movie but never read the first page of the novel. The Met Club, as it was often called, had been founded in 1891 (the era of horse-drawn carriages) and erected on land purchased from the Duchess of Marlborough. The architecture was exquisite. Inside, the tall marble columns leaped up at least fifteen feet from golden-white marble floors, accented with the lush, burgundy colors of the Club, which was also a very exclusive hotel. The atmosphere, although strictly formal in terms of sartorial taste, was quite relaxed and comfortable. The service was excellent, and unlike other clubs and restaurants who tried to substitute snobbery for excellence, The Met Club was a perfect place for engagements with business and social acquaintances. Business meetings were forbidden. However, social engagements with business acquaintances could be most enjoyable and relaxed. The main floor had been set half a level above the sidewalk and the big windows offered a nice view of Fifth Avenue, Central Park, and the city in general.

I awakened with more of the excitement of the previous day when, upon looking at the front page of *The New York Times*, I saw another story on the Russian nukes. It was the biggest news of the day. I checked in at my office on Fifth Avenue, made several phone calls and set several news and publishing meetings for the day. That done, I was quickly out on the street and on my way. It seemed like in New York I could wear the soles off a pair of shoes in a week, and it was imperative that my shoes fit well or one day could kill my feet. Walking was often faster than a cab if the meetings were all uptown; sometimes you could catch a cab and sometimes not. Cross-town traffic was usually impossible and cabs moved at less than the walking speed.

Today I was trying to catch a cab to get to West 57th, and passing a newsstand on the street I stopped and perused several newspapers to see how nuclear smuggling was being reported throughout the nation. But not all newspapers were running it front page, or even at all! *The Wall Street Journal.* had been very low key about it in comparison to the *Times*, and other papers like *The Chicago Tribune* and *The Denver Post* hardly printed anything, burying the story in the ninth or tenth pages. I hoped it wasn't a clue to my reception at the television stations.

I caught a cab and headed to my first meeting—at CBS.

My first appointment of the day was with a Connie Chung producer for *Eye to Eye*. It was a large building and their offices were fairly high in the building. I rode the elevator and anxiously entered their lobby for the show. Upon announcement, Gary Scurka came out to greet me. We shook hands and he invited me into his office.

"So you've got a book about the Russian nukes," he said getting right to the point.

"Yes, *The Moscow Connection* by Robin Moore," I replied and handed him a set of advance copy, bound galleys.

"Hmm. A novel. Fiction?"

"Faction. Fiction based on fact."

"Well, we're in the news business, not the fiction business."

"Of course, but fiction often tells the facts better than non-fiction. We've got the story of the Russian mafia moving into New York City and taking over Brighton Beach. Robin nicknamed the Russian godfather *the Jap* and the real-life godfather was just arrested here in the City. It's the first book on the Russian mafia selling plutonium and complete nuclear weapons to terrorist nations. Yesterday, that broke the hard news for the first time, and it's front-page news in *The New York Times* again today."

"Oh, I know, I know, *believe me*, I know it's true. What I'm trying to do is *prove* it."

"Then read the page proofs and interview the real people behind the story, like Peter Grinenko."

"Who's Peter Grinenko?"

I explained and Gary listened intently. Realizing I was getting long-winded, he suddenly said, "Excuse me for interrupting, but I've got an interview to go to and if I don't leave right now I'll miss it. Let me just say a few things here. First, I believe you on the nukes. In fact, I know it's true. I've been working on a related story for months." Gary then started telling me about a source he had who knew a lot about smuggling and loose nukes.

I stopped him mid-sentence. "I know who he is," I said.

Gary was shocked. "You know who he is?"

"Yes. He's in prison."

Gary's face flushed red and he shouted at me, "You better be careful how you answer this next question—you better tell me how you know that. Because all the court files are sealed by the judge for so-called national security—and if you're with the CIA or the government—I'll personally throw you the fuck right out of here!" I had heard later from a reliable source that the court files were not sealed, but I didn't have that information at the time, and besides, Gary was hopping mad! And he had even used the "f" word. That seemed out of his character, but I remembered something about character that I had learned from literary theory: try to ask yourself what special circumstances in life would cause you to behave exactly as the person you are ready to criticize. I could only wonder what he'd been through.

I looked at him calmly and said, "While Robin and I were editing *The Moscow Connection*, Robin asked me to take a break for a few minutes so he could write a very important letter he had promised. He explained that he was writing to the judge on a case to ask for leniency before sentencing. I also knew about your source from invitations he sent Robin and I over the last couple of years to participate in his International Arms Expo in Fayetteville. Robin always went but I couldn't fit it into my schedule, or I would know him personally."

"You know why he's in prison?"

"Robin told me wire fraud charges, but Robin also says he thinks he's innocent."

"Of course he's innocent. I'm trying to prove that here at CBS, but that's not why he's in prison. He's in prison because of what he knows about the Russians selling nuclear weapons. Not just plutonium, but complete nuclear weapons. Ever heard of backpack nukes, the ones that a hiker can carry around? The Secretary of Defense, the CIA, the FBI, they all deny that they even exist, let alone that Russian nukes are a threat to the world. My source not only says they exist, and that they have already been sold to terrorist nations, *he says he can prove it!*" Gary shouted those last words with the same fervor that he offered to throw me out of his office if I worked for the government.

"Wooowww," I said slowly, and softly, taking it all in, absolutely taking it all in, and also there was a twinge of fear. I knew the book I was publishing was the tip of the iceberg, and now I was sitting on the iceberg. Gary stared coolly, straight into my eyes, his blonde hair and blue eyes so intense that I could see the lightning with which Gary could work and strike, and I could see why he had risen as a television journalist to one of the top news shows in New York. The intensity held tight for just another moment as we regarded each other and measured our mutual reactions, and then Gary said softly, almost sadly, "I really do have to go. But I'm impressed that you knew about my source. He's in prison for what he knows. The scary thing is it could happen to any of us. I'll tell you the rest of the story after I follow up on your book. Give me Peter Grinenko's phone number and I'll call him. I'm not promising you *anything*, but I'll call him. I'll tell you one more thing before I go. You would not believe what I've been through—professionally—and personally— to keep this story alive—because it's so hot, and the government is trying so hard, to keep it out of the news, that nothing they do at this point would surprise me. And you—working on the same stuff—better be ready for the same thing. Be ready. It ain't pretty." He paused for a moment and the feeling of strangeness I'd had on the plane mixed with what I'd just heard.

I had nothing to do with Gary Scurka's source or his case. So my knowledge is and was, at the time, quite limited. I had never met him, and I don't mean to pass judgment on the accuracy of Gary Scurka's comments regarding his source or the government denying the existence of backpack nukes at the time. I'm only recounting my conversation with Gary and how he described his experiences to me. It affected me. He was passionate, and furious, and it certainly made me wonder what I should expect. However, I must add that I had never, to date, been directly or physically abused or harassed by any government official. I found solace in that, and felt that it was a credit to my government that I had not, yet I kept very alert as I went forward with *The Moscow Connection*.

I didn't say anything, I just looked at him. He was still thinking. Then he continued.

"Now, if I can help you in any way, I will. And thanks for coming in. Now, I'm late and I'm rushing out of here, but make yourself at home here in my office, make some calls if you'd like, feel free to use the phone, or the copy machine, whatever. Jay, it's a pleasure to meet you."

He put out his hand and we shook. And he was gone.

I was still stunned, for two reasons: first, the subject matter just revealed to me, which triggered memories of past government interference with my life trying to stop the book I published about Cuba, and second, I felt I had met a true journalist. I wondered what he'd been through and what had been done to him, partly so that I could brace myself for more of the same. I'd met numerous producers and news-media professionals and must admit that many of those people appeared superficial in their jobs. I wondered how many of them would take a stand against a story being repressed for political or government reasons. That was the cutting edge. Were these people just going through the motions of news? Are they really true to the art? Would any of them take a stand if it meant a risk of losing their job? After all, without their big news company behind them, what were they? Without a big company producing and broadcasting their programs, as individuals, they were nothing.

I took Gary's warning to heart as I left the CBS building and headed down the street to ABC to meet Christopher Harper, a producer of *20/20*. I wondered what would happen there, thinking back that I had known Chris over the phone for about a year, and I had just met him two weeks ago in person. We talked then about *The Moscow Connection* and he had expressed great interest in the story, telling me to come back in a week or two and he would see what he could do.

My high hopes were tempered somewhat by my meeting at CBS, but Chris had expressed interest before the story broke front-page in *The New York Times*. Surely, now, he would do a story for television. It was the hottest news of the day!

I held that thought as I entered his office and shook his hand. Chris greeted me with a big smile and invited me to sit down. Then he sat down himself, a big, gregarious man with a pleasant face and a black suit and white shirt and red tie, much the same way I was dressed.

"I don't have anything good to tell you," he said, matter-of-factly.

"You don't believe it?"

"It's not that *I* don't believe it. I *always* believed it, and you, from the first time we met." He just stopped with that and sat there looking at me.

I broke the silence. "Then what is it?"

Chris pointed his finger up into the air.

I could only guess. "What, God won't let you do this story?"

"No. Administration. I want to do this story. I have wanted to do a similar story for months. They won't let me do it."

"But you're the producer."

"I can't do anything if they tell me not to."

I took a deep breath. My enthusiasm flowed into the floor, and my eyes went to the floor along with it. Suddenly I became so angry that I couldn't have spoken without shouting. I just kept it inside for a few moments, and then I spoke very evenly and deliberately, although it must have sounded like I could easily have broken into a rage.

"Chris, let me tell you something. Robin Moore went to Russia off and on for two years to get this story. He was invited by the Chief of Militsia in Moscow and the story grew from there. He's been to secret cities, he's interviewed Chechins, he's been inside several of their prisons, he's seen Russia and its people in a way that's very rare. And none of the big houses in New York will touch it. They want to do *their* version of Russia, something that fits *their list*, as if there is a consensus of how Americans should write about Russia and what they should read. The fact is, there's no realism in it. It's all a *party line.* Well, they can publish what they want, but if the news only covers *their* books—"

"I know what you mean. I have a problem with that myself."

"Their party line is bubble gum! And the front-page news today proves it."

"Jay, you're preaching to the choir. But unfortunately, none of what you're saying is going to get into ABC, at least not through this program. I sympathize with you, I really do."

That was it. He was done. I was done. No matter how you conjugated it, it was done. I shrugged my shoulders. I was running out of gestures. I was out of smooth exits in hopes of a future book and future stories. I looked at the floor, thinking. I started to get up out of my chair, and he held out his arm.

"Let me add something before you go. This is all very disturbing to me. I don't like the way the programs have been going, and I don't see us doing much of what I call real news. I don't get to do a lot of stuff that I want to do."

"Thanks, Chris. It means more than you think. Maybe you don't get to do real news but at least you're a real person, a real journalist. At least you perceive it. It's a headless monster, surrounded by all its minions, and it raises the question, *Who is running the news?*"

That was it. The meeting ended and I thanked him for his time. There was nothing really more to discuss. Two powerless people talking about what was not going to appear on a major news network was not a topic to dwell on. And I struggled with my energy level as I hit, once again, the street. I said a few select words to myself, aloud, and a passerby gave me a glance like, *well, there's another one talking to himself.*

I realized how I must have looked and decided to go into a nearby café where I sat down, ordered coffee, and put some sugar in it. What a bunch of bullshit.

I had to think my way out of this funk because it was all on me. I couldn't even look to the sky. I liked to do that, look at clouds or blue sky, or mountains. So I looked at the street instead.

It was the Upper West Side. An endless stream of people flowed by me—carried by the energy of lives in a city full of energy—flowing as if one—yet dodging, cutting around each other, anything to keep from breaking stride—because they're really not part of each other. They don't move like a school of fish who all turn in unison at the same instant. They move like green leaves floating on a stream. When the water changes they all jam up, only comfortable standing close together if it means crowding up behind someone, as if that will help move them forward. Somehow I had to transcend the flow of the news and get inside the picture. Not as a leaf on the stream, but inside, where the water comes from.

Obviously there was major power and major force operating against publicity or even acknowledgement in the news of the Russian nuke problem. Gary Scurka had broached the subject directly, Christopher Harper had alluded to it, and I had experienced similar forces in the past on some of my other books which were politically sensitive to the government. I had seen what I thought were the effects of government opposition. So, was it totally the government behind it?

I had a friend in New York who produced high-level corporate commercials and, like me, had recently opened an office in New York. I'd been meaning to call him during this visit but hadn't yet. So, just on the moment, I did.

He was in. "Tom!"

"Jay!"

"I'm in the city." I already felt better. He always had good energy.

"Yes? So what's new? I don't have much time, but I've always got a minute for you, pal. What's up?"

"I'm doing publicity on my book about Russia."

"How's it going?"

"It's not."

"Are you surprised?"

"You're damned right I'm surprised. I've got the only book on Russian nukes in the black market, it's front page news in the *Times*, and I can't get a single television interview for the author?"

"Are you surprised?"

"Yes! It's the news, dammit. What are they doing?"

"Jay, that's your problem. You think it's *news*."

"Of course, I mean, what else?"

"Jay. It's not *news*. Now get this word: ready, set, it's—*entertainment*."

"Oh, come on, man, CBS News, ABC News, all the evening news programs, what are you talking about?"

"What's CNN?"

"The *cable news network*."

"No. Try again."

"That's what CNN stands for."

"No. Listen to the program. It's the *entertainment* news network."

"Hm. You know, I've heard that. And now that I think about it, it just didn't click. Man, I didn't even think of it that way. That's bullshit."

"But that's the way it is. Don't think of it as *news*. It's not. That's where your idealism is screwing with your head. Get real."

"Okay, you make a good point. So Americans are screwed if they think they're getting news on TV. So it's entertainment, which makes me want to puke. So what drives it? I've got to get inside—inside the stream."

"The stream?"

"Never mind. A metaphor. What drives the news, I mean, entertainment?"

"It's real easy. It's what drives my business: corporate dollars."

"I've got to think on that one."

"Hey, Bimbo, I'm not picking on you, and I've really got to go. Think about it, and call me at the hotel later if you want. You know where I'm at."

"Thanks Tom. It's disgusting."

"It's real."

Back at my table I watched the people streaming by the window on the sidewalk but I didn't really see them. I saw a collage, with floating images—government—corporate dollars—politicians—television—newspapers. The ideas blended—I was searching for words to describe relationships—okay—government regulates industry—politics decide international business—Russia was new business—yet to be defined—US government regulations—US government policy on Russia—invest? Where's the money? Whose money?

The Russian government was broke. So there's no money there. The Russian military was collapsed. Was it really? Well, would they really just roll over? Or were the nukes going out to terrorist nations for a reason? Was the cold war simply taking a new, secret direction?

It came back to the money. Stability. That's why—I could only guess—Americans were not to know about the nukes going to terrorist nations. Somehow, I became convinced, somebody was going to make a ton of money off the collapse of the Soviet Union. Where the money would come from, I hadn't figured out yet. And that would be the key. That would tell me why Robin's book was denied in the press. And his book wasn't only about the nukes. It was about organized crime taking over major businesses in Russia. It was about the new Russian government in *partnership* with Russian crime bosses. And the Russian crime bosses were getting filthy rich. So where would US corporate dollars come into play? I couldn't figure that out. But that word—*partnership*—hung in my mind. It dawned on me that the relationship between the US government and large US corporations seemed more like partnership than regulation. I considered all the mergers I had recently seen, banks, oil companies, especially publishers, merging, being acquired. Partnership. Boy, you want to talk about power. The richest, most powerful corporations in the world in partnership with the richest, most powerful government in the world—now that's power. Who could possibly get a foot in edgewise? Or even a word?

Obviously, there was some major power operating against publicity or even acknowledgement of the Russian nuke problem. Just in one day, Gary Scurka and Christopher Harper had both complained about it, and there were my own experiences—especially regarding Cuba. To me, there was no justification for it. Freedom to publish was freedom to publish. Period. Free writing and reading—especially about politics—could have no limits in a democracy. I felt that I had the right—the *duty*—to publish Robin's book and if the government—or anybody—was going to interfere with the flow of information on the subject—then I just had to work harder to get the book out. And fight them.

Energy level back on track, I decided to contact the editor of *The New York Times Book Review*. I had tried to call in the past, and once got the direct phone number into Rebecca Sinkler's office. In the way that fate and luck sometimes favor an event as if it is destiny, Rebecca herself answered the phone. Apparently her secretary hadn't come in yet, so she had picked up when I rang.

Expecting her secretary, I said, "Hello. This is Jay Fraser. I'm the publisher with Affiliated Writers of America from Wyoming. Is Rebecca Sinkler in?"

"This is."

Equally abrupt and surprised, I said, "Good morning. First, I'd like to thank all of you at the *Book Review* for the kind review of our first hardcover."

"Which book was that?"

"*Leave Me My Spirit* by Lawrence Lunt, who spent fourteen years in Cuban prisons."

"I remember that."

"You do?"

"Yes, I do. And it's interesting that you called because I just got back from Yellowstone a couple of weeks ago."

"Wonderful. How'd you like it?"

"Beautiful."

It was an interesting irony, and we talked about Wyoming a bit, and then the conversation came around to books. I said, "I've submitted other books since Lunt's book, but haven't been fortunate enough for any more reviews. But I'm hoping my next one will be important enough. Would you have time today that I might hand you the page proofs in person?"

"We don't generally allow publishers in here."

"Oh. Well, this book is about the sale of nuclear weapons on the black market, which is front-page news today, and I must tell you that I have concerns that the page proofs I submit may not get where they need to. If I hand them to you, at least I know you got them."

She laughed, but in a polite way. "Do you know how many submissions we get every week?"

"Thousands?"

"Do you know how many books we review per week?"

"Forty?"

"Close. Twenty."

"So I should figure my odds, right?"

"If you've had one review, how many submissions have you made?"

I was embarrassed. "Ten," I said meekly.

"You're way ahead of the odds."

I didn't have much left in my voice after having to admit how small my company was. And now I felt even smaller than that. It seemed hopeless. But I said, in one last desperate try, "Well, then let me put it this way. If you never review another book I publish, I'll understand. Really, I will. But please, look at this one. Let me bring it to you so I know it at least got delivered. Some haven't, you know."

Much to my surprise, she said okay, and she set a time.

CHAPTER FOUR
Developing Pre-Publication Allies

In addition to publicity, I had other business that was paramount. I had decided to print *The Moscow Connection* with Berryville Graphics, located in Berryville, Virginia, just a short drive from Washington Dulles Airport. It was owned by Bertelsman, a German firm and the largest printing company in the world—the largest book publisher in the world—who bought three very large publishers in New York—Bantam, Doubleday and Dell—combining them into one huge "house" called Bantam, Doubleday, Dell—BDD to us in the trade—and also owning major interests in related industries which at the time I had no knowledge of. The logo for my company was AWA and they had printed several of my titles in the past. They knew AWA books and wanted to know me, personally, even to the point that when I was on my way to Europe and had a connection in DC, the president of Berryville Graphics sent his personal secretary to meet me and give me gifts for myself and my children. I must have been somewhat of a mystery to them—owners of so many huge publishing houses—and here's this little guy from Wyoming doing national and international books. Usually I visited a printing facility either prior to or during the first print run, just to meet them and see their equipment. I hadn't been to Berryville yet, but assumed that at some point in time I would.

I contacted Berryville Graphics from The Met Club in New York and arranged for them to bid the book according to the page count and hardcover specifications. They also recommended a dustjacket design firm they said was good and easy to work with. Time was essential so I decided to go with their recommendation. I told them the print run would be 25,000 to 50,000 copies, exact quantity to be determined at the last possible moment—based on the strength of advance reviews and advance purchases.

That done, I called Baker & Taylor, the second-largest book wholesaler in America, and my best wholesale account. The wholesaler in American book distribution was the most critical channel of sales for a small publisher such as AWA wishing to produce mass-market, trade hardcover books. The chain stores, Waldenbooks and all the ones that Barnes & Noble owns, will not buy directly from a small publisher. Even though the buyers at the chains worked one-on-one with me to order books—they would not *buy* the books from me. I had to sell to a wholesaler—one which they will *buy* from—in order to get my books into the chains. So without an accepted wholesaler, I would have no chainstore sales, or even to many of the 20,000 independent bookstores in America. Most bookstores order from wholesalers, and if their *preferred wholesaler* doesn't carry the book, they simply don't buy it, even if a customer asks for it.

My buyer at Baker & Taylor, Jean Swope, took my call and quickly realized the potential of *The Moscow Connection*. She became excited and we talked about the possibility of it becoming a best seller. I gave her the ISBN number and other pertinent information over the phone, and she told me she would enter the title in their database, and also agreed to be vendor of record with the chainstores, assuring me that she would work with me to get inventories in on time to meet demand. This meant that everything was in place for distribution of the book.

I went after advance sales aggressively, armed with front-page news and ongoing questions of global nuclear security and Russian mafia activity in New York. I called the national buyer at Waldenbooks in Stamford, Connecticut (soon to move to Michigan when K-Mart bought them), and Jim Duffy had no problem making Baker & Taylor vendor of record on the book, and was very interested. The vendor of record is the wholesaler which is designated in a chainstore database which tells the buyers and clerks at every store where to order the book if there is demand or a request for a special order. I promised him page proofs right away so he could read it. I did the same thing with Barnes & Noble, although I was a bit unsure at first, because Sessalee Hensley had refused to buy from Baker & Taylor in the past. But to my happy discovery, things had changed, she said Barnes & Noble would buy from Baker & Taylor, and she set it up that way. She wanted several sets of page proofs for several other buyers. Sessalee Hensley was then, and still is today, one of the most powerful people in America regarding the success of fiction books, and she has been the subject of national news many times. Her buying relationship with me was very, very important.

Thusly, the printing, dustjacket art, wholesale distribution, and chainstore market channel was set. The promotion had a good start, and now I could again focus on trying to get major reviews and national news on the book.

I was unable to get through to Manuella Hoelterhoff at *The Wall Street Journal.*, so the best I could do was send her a set of pageproofs Fed-Ex and then follow up on the phone.

I was able, however, to meet with some of the staff at *Publishers Weekly* and *Library Journal* in New York City, and that was interesting since several of AWA's books had been reviewed by both magazines in the past.

Eventually, personal letters and advance bound galleys went out to over fifty major newspapers, networks, and magazines throughout the USA.

CHAPTER FIVE
The Russian-American: Act Two

"He says you're full of shit!"

"What?"

"Peter Grinenko says you're full of shit! Says you and Robin Moore and the book are full of shit."

The brevity of what I was hearing from Gary Scurka at CBS in New York sank in hard and deep. There was no instant answer. I was actually in shock, and could barely even muster up a voice I was suddenly so weak. I was weary of being blindsided and here it was again.

"That's not what he told me."

"That doesn't surprise me."

"What?"

"It doesn't surprise me. I've been through it. I've been through the same thing. Ever since I started working on the story about my source and backpack nukes, the same thing has been happening to discredit me. Look. When you're dealing with news on Russian nukes, you are dealing with the most sensitive information in the world. The world, Jay. You wouldn't believe—well, you probably would—but I've been through pure hell with this case. And I'm not giving up. I'm not giving up! I know I'm right and I'll stake my whole career on it."

"Well—I'm going to call Peter and tell him exactly what you said."

"Good."

I picked up the phone and dialed anxiously. I heard the line click open and asked to speak to Peter.

"This is Peter."

"Jay Fraser here. Did you tell Gary Scurka that Robin and I are full of shit?"

"Ye—es." The word was drawn out, like a piece of gooey, bubblegum stretched out slowly from his mouth, but also present in that spoken word was his usual, jovial, cocky tone.

I was silent for a moment. "Did you tell me the opposite?"

"Ye—es." Still the same tone.

"What the hell are you doing?" I shouted. I was furious.

"It's not personal," Peter said.

"The hell it's not. You tell Robin and me one thing, and tell the news the opposite?"

"That's right."

"Why?"

"Look. The book is fiction."

"I'm not talking about the book now. I'm talking about Peter Grinenko telling me one thing and telling the opposite to the news."

"Okay."

"Not okay. Why did you do this?"

"It's my job."

"Noooooo. Nooooo. You're shittin' me! You're working for the agency now?"

"Yep."

"I guess Robin fictionalized you pretty well as the main character. It got you a job, eh? Well, good for you. If this is true, then it's not personal. But it's disgusting. You've been bought. What about the truth? What about news? I don't believe you. Prove it to me."

"I will."

"How?"

"You want to see my 1099?"

"Yes."

"Okay. I'll fax it to you."

"Jeez, Peter. I told you that you'd be famous because of this book. It didn't take long for them to come, did it?"

"Nope."

"Good luck."

"You too."

A few minutes later the fax came and there it was, full flush in the face. It was the end of that part of the story. Gawd, I still liked him. You couldn't help it. He was charismatic and charming and—and—at least he was honest with me—at the personal level. Not counting the double talk, that is. At least he had given me the reason. He didn't have to do that. Maybe he wanted to.

"Gary, I talked with Peter. He works for the agency now."

"So? I'm not surprised."

"Does anything surprise you?"

"Yes. A lot of things. Like—why didn't the FBI use their regular handwriting analyst to get an opinion in the lab on the signature on my scource's wire fraud documents? They did on every other case in the recent past, but not this one."

"Hmm. Who did they use?"

"No one! As near as I can tell. But, of course, they're not cooperating with me. They don't want me on this story. And they're doing everything they can to hide things from me."

Robin Moore was back in Boston and I called him there at his home. "Robin. Jay here. Guess what?"

"What?"

"Peter Grinenko told Gary Scurka at CBS that the book is shit, that we're full of shit."

"Good heavens, I don't know why he would do that. Why would he do such a thing?"

"He's literally working for the agency now."

"Really?"

"Really. I didn't believe it either until he sent me his 1099."

"He has a lot of input to this story. I mean, he is the main character."

"And you've done his character well. When I met him, I felt like I already knew him. This switch in his story, however, is not good."

"No, it's not. But there's nothing we can do about it now. I better have a talk with him right away."

"Good. But I don't know what good it will do."

"I don't either."

I thought for a moment and then asked, "You coming to New York?"

"Yes. I'll be there tomorrow morning. We're having lunch with the Duke. So plan on it. I'll meet you at the club when I get there from the airport."

"We going to Hoboken?"

"No, he's coming into the City. I want you to meet some of the FBI guys; they'll be there."

"Interesting," I replied, not about to mix Gary Scurka's experience with the FBI with the lunch.

"I think it will be. Jimmy Fox cracked the World Trade Center bombing case. He will be there. And you'll like the Duke."

CHAPTER SIX
The Birth, or Death, of a Book

The New York Times Book Review offices were up the elevator in the building. Rebecca Sinkler greeted me cordially and we shook hands. I had a curious yet reverent regard for her—the head of the most prestigious book review in the world. Her demeanor was very personal and yet elegant, and she spoke with me in very normal tones, ushering me through and showing me the various phases of the quite large operation. She was attractive and sincere, making me at once feel at ease. She seemed very humble about her work—I think she wanted me to see the guts of how it works. It was a great compliment she had given to even meet me—let alone take me through the department. I wondered why she had done it. I was really nobody in the publishing world—just a little company from of all places—Wyoming. Maybe it was just that I was trying—maybe it was something in the books I was doing—sometimes when you get a break in life you wonder why—even while it's still happening.

She literally took the time to walk me on a tour and explain in detail every phase and aspect of how a book comes in, goes through the various stages of reading and/or assignment to a potential reviewer (usually an expert on the topic or genre of the book), and either winds up as *one of the twenty a week*, or *in one of the many dumpsters* strategically placed throughout the areas to enable that sad end of the function. It must have made them feel like a publisher feels when they have to reject a manuscript.

"I live in Philadelphia, and commute," she said, explaining that the train ride enabled her to meet her vast requirements for reading. I felt that her point blank honesty was surprising, and very pleasant. In my mind I compared her to others in the business who seem to hide behind brittle facades to survive, seemingly unable to function in this kind of candor.

"Here's the book," I offered, holding it in my hand. She took it and promptly put it on the shelf among the other books that come in, signifying an instant sense of ethics about the book. It was a big set of shelves, and there were at least several hundred books on it, maybe even thousands. There were certainly thousands in the system, and it was all very well organized. The way it was run brought a sense of fairness to mind that was impeccable.

We talked a while longer, some about Yellowstone, but I didn't want to overstay my welcome.

We parted on a good note. "Thank you," I said quietly, adding, "This means a lot to me."

I could tell by her countenance that she could see that I was somewhat dazed, and I was, and couldn't have hidden it even if I'd wanted to. The experience had been like seeing a great painting—not the lithograph—the painting. Honesty begets honesty. I knew I was a young publisher, I was a bit dazed, had a lot to learn, and right then, I learned a very good deal.

"You got into *The New York Times Book Review*?" Robin nearly spilled his drink at the table as we sat near his favorite window at The Met Club.

The way Robin blurted it out startled me—he was shocked—I was abashed—because I had so much respect for Rebecca Sinkler and the *Book Review*.

My response was much more measured. "She decided to see me. It was quite an honor."

"How did you do it?"

"I called her number and her secretary was not there yet and she answered the phone herself. We spoke a while and we set a meeting. Your book is there. I took it personally—it's in the system. So at least we know they got it. But I must also tell you that I was able to speak with Manuella Hoelterhoff, and she didn't receive her review copy. She said she'd remember that kind of book if she saw it."

"Hoelterhoff?"

"*Wall Street Journal.*"

"Oh yes, of course, the arts page editor, she didn't get it? How did you send it?"

"Fed Ex, overnight, but it doesn't matter."

"Yes it does, you can get a signature."

"No it doesn't. It won't mean anything. I've got the signature—from Fed Ex—Mary Hanson. What good is a signature from a mail room at an organization that large? You could spend a whole week trying to track it all down and prove who took it out of the system, and you'd never get inside that giant newspaper to do that. It's a red herring. I told Manuella I'd send her another copy."

"Too bad you can't go meet her."

"Yes, I know. She's in DC. Best we can do is send another copy."

Robin was resolute. "We can't let them stop this book."

"I know. I'm doing the best I can. I wish I could just get a better understanding about who *they* are. I mean names, people actually doing something. Proof."

"Well, keep working on it. They tried to stop *The Green Berets*, you know. Kennedy was dead and Johnson didn't want Americans to read the truth about Vietnam."

A bitterness came to his voice as he began to tell the story. Kennedy wanted the public to know what we were doing there, and what the French were doing, and he agreed to send Robin to Vietnam to write a book. Robin went through training as a Green

Beret, the only civilian to ever do so, and he went to Vietnam in 1964 to write about the war.

But things had changed at the White House. Kennedy had been assassinated and Johnson became president. Johnson wanted to escalate the war and didn't want the book to be published. Crown had agreed to publish the book in 1965, but suddenly there was Pentagon ire, supposedly because the book gave away military secrets, but actually because the book glorified the Green Berets. The National Security Agency threatened to arrest Robin and shut down the Crown publication set for April 1965 for violating the War Secrets Act. It was a hot fight, and a writer who had been wounded and crippled from WWII was working for *The New York Times* and wrote a story which the *Times* ran, and which helped save Robin from arrest and the book from censorship.

Moore was called into the Pentagon where General Underwood showed Robin a copy of his book with eighteen red tabs sticking out of it. Moore was told that each tab represented top secret "need to know only" information. Moore was shocked, since there was nothing in the book which wasn't well-known by the enemy or anyone else who took the trouble to go out where the war was being fought. Moore said to Underwood, "I can't believe that. Let me have a look."

The General grabbed the book and snapped, "This book is classified."

Ultimately, it was Gerald Ford who saved Robin and the book. He had heard of the attempted censorship by the Pentagon and simply read the eighteen "top secret" passages into the Congressional Record, thusly "declassifying them" and killing any chance for Moore or the publisher to be prosecuted. The book sold 600,000 copies in hardcover alone, and by fall of 1965 it was number one on *The New York Times* bestseller list.

I listened patiently, intently, feeling the emotion build up about our present situation, and then said, "I know the story, Robin."

"Well, they're doing it again. We've got to get this book out. Now listen. Charles Hanley at *Associated Press* here in New York wants to speak with you; they're going to do a news story and want to see page proofs. Also, Cindy Adams with the *Post* interviewed me for a story, and she wants to interview you as well. So we're getting *some* news. Jay, we've got to keep going. And you're doing a good job of it. *The New York Times Book Review*? I think it's good that they showed you around."

The Duke had invited us to lunch at Kennedy's. Kennedy's was a lively Irish pub on West 57th, and the restaurant and bar at the back were elegantly decorated with lots of green and white tablecloths for the Irish decor. The walls were lavishly paneled with rich, dark wood. Most of the staff looked Irish and sounded Irish, and probably were, especially Maurice, the bartender.

Seated for lunch at a long table against the far wall were a number of large-bodied men in suits: the FBI of New York. I pegged them instantly, and also could plainly see who would have been the Duke, who, seated at the head of the table, caught a glimpse of Robin with his quick eyes as soon as we came into view as we walked toward the bar where Maurice was bartender.

Robin introduced me as his publisher and the Duke looked me over carefully and fully—late thirties or early forties in age, tall and lean, bright blue eyes and sandy brown hair, hawk nose which obviously had been broken, wearing a suit but not a fine suit by New York standards, barely what you'd even call a suit by the Duke's impression, and the Duke knew suits. After all, he was in the clothing business in Hoboken. It was his clothing warehouse that Robin had created the scene in the book about. The Duke, Joe Kohler was his name but we called him the Duke, was buying pallets of clothes from stores who wanted to dump inventory, and then selling the clothes to Russian immigrants for very cheap prices. Brand new clothes for ten cents on the dollar. The Russians were brought to the warehouse on buses. So Robin wrote about it in the book.

Come on over and meet the guys," the Duke said.

Robin sat at the head of one end of the table, and the Duke stood beside him and introduced him, then introduced me, and then returned to his seat at the other end of the long table. I sat in the middle with the FBI agents. Robin ordered gin and tonic, I ordered white wine, and the FBI agents ordered beer. The Duke was quick to get to the heart of the matter at hand.

"Jay! Tell us what it *means* to be a publisher."

"It means we select a manuscript from the many which are submitted, buy it from the author, edit it, manufacture it, and put it out on the market." As I said the words *buy it* I could see in the Duke's face that the Duke knew there had been only a token advance paid to Robin. The Duke was indirect in his response.

"Is that what an *advance* is, when you buy it?"

"Advance against royalties. Sometimes authors get paid a large sum of money up front. My company doesn't do this. We don't have that kind of capital. But we do have enough capital to pay a small advance, print the book in quantity, and get it out into the market. We promise that we'll do our best in that regard."

"What do you do to get it into the market?"

"It is probably one of the most complex and difficult markets in the world. But I can't possibly explain the complexities of the book market over lunch"—I looked around the table and at Robin—"and it would bore everyone else at the table."

"Oh, I don't know about that. We're very interested in Robin's book. And—after all—I'm in it! I want it to succeed!" He laughed raucously and then continued. "Where can we get the book when it comes out?"

With that question, I paused. I looked around and I had the attention of the whole table. Calmly, and with total confidence, I smiled and said, "Just go to any Waldenbooks or Barnes & Noble Store. They'll have it, or be able to get it. It's in their systems already. That's all set."

Everyone respected the chain stores as a measure of a publisher's credibility. They all nodded, and with that answer they were all comfortable that the publication of the book was real.

There was a toast to Robin and the book, and then the conversation shifted into easy and interesting discussions about New York City and crime and all sorts of topics. Time went by smoothly, everyone seeming to enjoy the meal and a few drinks, and then suddenly—like it always does in a busy city—time became an issue.

"Well, gotta go," the Duke declared abruptly to everyone, then to me, "Come on over to Hoboken. You need to see the warehouse when the Russians come in. Forty-four long? I'll see what I got. If I don't have anything, I can order it."

Robin and I took a cab back to The Met Club and it was hot in the late-afternoon sun. Once inside, we were exhausted. We'd both been running full tilt with little rest since the day we signed the book together and we decided to go downstairs to the health club and take steam saunas, hoping that would refresh our bodies and give us some time for mental rest. Before I could do that, I had a lot to do right then. I asked Robin to go ahead and I'd be down in a few minutes. Then I went up to the room and returned the call to *Associated Press*, and luckily I got Charles Hanley on the phone. He interviewed me right then and there on the phone, and immediately after hanging up I addressed a Fed-Ex package to overnight him the page proofs. That done, I put calls in to several editors at major New York publishing houses to discuss selling them the paperback rights. My company was a hardcover publisher, and paperback publishing was an entirely different printing and marketing system for distribution. There was quite an interest from several editors, and I sent several sets of page proofs out to them as well. I also made several appointments to meet some of them in person. With that much done, I felt content and relaxed that I'd put in the best day I physically could. Now I could go meet Robin in the sauna.

I went downstairs and got out of my suit and grabbed a towel. I didn't see Robin so I went into the steam sauna. He was still in there, soaking up the steam and relaxing—as the heat stimulated his circulation and flushed his body fluids through his bloodstream and organs. I got in and stayed longer than he did and it felt great.

I got out and sat down in a chair next to Robin, both of us drenched in sweat.

"What do you think of the Duke?" Robin asked.

"Gets right to the point."

"Wait till you see the warehouse. Quite a set up he's got there—pallets and pallets of clothes and hats. Every kind of clothing—shirts, pants, jeans, suits—he buys the stuff by the truckloads for pennies on the dollar and then brings these Russian immigrants in on buses. Like on a Saturday, full busloads of them, sets up a keg of beer, and the Russians go on a rampage. Usually they buy all they can carry. It's really a sight to behold."

"The scene in the book describes it well. He's invited me to come over and see it myself, and I plan to. Obviously he's making money off the Russians. And other people are, too, I'm very sure of that. I've been thinking a lot about the relationship between big business and government in America—in my opinion it's a partnership—and I'll just bet you that there's a business connection—a huge business connection—behind all this fake news. That's the real 'Moscow Connection' and it's bigger money than black market nukes." Gawd, it hit me like a brick in the face. That had to be it. "Somebody with tremendous power in the government is making big deals over there that are not public and using their power to influence the media."

"You may be onto something there, Jay. The Russian mafia and the Russian government is a partnership, too. The privatization process is chaos—nobody knows who owns anything over there—it's all up for grabs."

I thought for a moment, and then said, "It will only be real journalists who find the real stories. And if the real stories can't get out—I'm afraid all of this is going to come back to haunt us. Our book is one piece in the mosaic, but it's not the whole picture—it's not even the biggest piece—unless of course—some terrorist starts *using* the nukes on America."

CHAPTER SEVEN
Beginning with the End

The next few days were more of the same. The arrest of the Russian nuke couriers was still front-page news, and the Cindy Adams story ran in the *New York Post*. Also a short article went out over the *Associated Press* wire about the book and about Affiliated Writers of America. The momentum was building in the news and as the days went by, there was more and more attention to the book. I sent more and more press packets and page proofs out, hitting all the major networks and talk shows. An editor from *The Library Journal* called and informed me that *The Moscow Connection* had been chosen as the feature book review for the November issue, and they requested the dustjacket art so they could illustrate the review with a full-color picture of the dustjacket. Then the *Associated Press* book review went out over the wire to practically every newspaper, network, and news agency in America.

In spite of all this, Larry King's producer, Pat Piper, declined to have Robin Moore on Larry King's CNN show to talk about the book. So I still couldn't crack anything on that magical TV power over Americans. I seemed to be doing well in the print media and even radio, but never TV. However, the producer for *The Jim Bohannon Show* (formerly the *Larry King Live* radio show) agreed to have Robin on for a live show, which was broadcast through The Mutual Broadcasting Network and would go out over 350 radio stations coast to coast.

Jim Duffy, the buyer at Waldenbooks, was enthusiastic about the book's potential sales volume and confirmed to me an initial order of 3,000 copies for over a thousand stores, coast to coast, which would be placed to Baker & Taylor electronically. Jim told me the order would go out the following Monday.

The buyers at Barnes & Noble confirmed a similar sized order, also for over 1,000 stores coast to coast, also to be sent electronically to Baker & Taylor. I'd hoped for bigger orders from the chains, but it was still a good start. I informed Robin of all of this, and also that when he went on autographing tours on the east coast that he should tell the bookstores to order copies of the book from Baker & Taylor.

At this point, I felt as though I had done the best job I could. The production, the publicity, the chain store orders, the distribution, it all seemed in place. I began to relax. I needed it. It had been non-stop stress and going twenty hours a day in New York.

I went back to Wyoming to spend some time at home.

Back in my office in Wyoming on Monday, that hot summer of 1994, I fielded numerous phone calls about the book and tried my best to catch up on all the other work which had piled up. The next day, Tuesday, I called Jean Swope, my buyer at Baker & Taylor, and asked if the chain store orders had come through electronically yet.

"No demand," she said.

"That's impossible. Jim Duffy, for one, told me the Waldenbooks order would go to you Monday."

"Zero demand. We didn't get the order."

I waited a few more days, which went by quickly since I was so far behind on my other work, and also enjoyed the time with my kids, and then I called her again.

"Zero demand," Jean Swope said, and the words hit me like ice. Neither Waldenbooks nor Barnes & Noble had orders for even a single book appearing in the Baker & Taylor system.

I began to feel sick. I could feel something wrong. It was like what happened when I was trying to get the book on Cuba out years ago, and suddenly all these things, inexplicably, happened. I resisted the fears, and the empty, sick feelings which grew inside of me—just like they had then—and just like they were doing now. Yet I knew that no matter how much I tried to say to myself that everything would be all right, it wouldn't be all right, and there was truly something seriously, seriously wrong. In all my years of publishing, when a buyer for a chain store confirms an order, you can take it to the bank. It always came through to the wholesaler as stated to the publisher. It was the way we did business.

So I knew something was seriously wrong, but I damned sure didn't want to make it worse by hounding the buyers at the chains. So I decided to give it more time. But it caused me stress every moment that it was up in the air, and made me wonder constantly what the hell was going on.

The next thing I knew, the deadline to set the quantity of the print run for *The Moscow Connection* was upon me, and literally all the advance orders for the book were still up in the air, or worse, had magically disappeared. I didn't know what the hell to do; I wasn't quite ready yet to stir it up at the chains, so, I cut the quantity of the print run from 25,000 or 50,000 copies, to a meager 12,000 copies. I told Berryville Graphics 12,000 copies because I still had this haunting feeling that something was going on—something weird was going on with those book orders.

In the middle of this, I got a fax copy of the image which our design firm had sent to *The Library Journal* to be used for their full-color article on *The Moscow Connection*, and it was the wrong image! It was completely wrong. Some idiot had sent the image of an earlier draft of the cover—which had been rejected—rather than the actual cover we decided on. I had to call the editor at *The Library Journal* and apologize (for someone else's mistake) and beg them to give me a day or two to get the right artwork sent to them as a replacement. I then discovered that I was taking them past *their* production deadline for the issue, a problem I was all too familiar with myself. I succeeded in getting it all done, however, and they accommodated me, but it strained all the personal relationships involved, which I didn't like one bit. And the stress of it all lingered and mixed with that of the orders which I *still* had not been able to locate.

Weeks went by and still "no demand" at Baker & Taylor. And then, magically, in contrast, Berryville Graphics called and informed me that the print run was finished early and ahead of the schedule they had given me, the books were done and ready to ship, and where did I want them sent? It would have been fantastic news if all my orders weren't disappearing.

I had planned to ship them straight to the Baker & Taylor warehouses to save the freight of shipping them to my warehouse in Wyoming and then back to the east coast. The books get torn up every time they get shipped, and then there's the double freight. Freight was expensive, and this was semi-truckloads of books going halfway across the country, so I just decided to leave them with the printer until I got things straightened out.

All this "demand" and books ready to ship and no place to ship them? It forced me to get after the root of the problem, the deep underlying problem—which had now suddenly reared its ugly head in a way which demanded confrontation.

I finally got through to Jim Duffy at Waldenbooks, busy now buying books for the next season. "Baker & Taylor says they never got the order."

"I sent it. It went out electronically."

"Can you just check and see why it didn't get to them?" It was a big favor to ask and I could feel my relationship with one of the most important buyers in America slipping, but I was trapped and had to do it.

He got back to me quickly and confirmed that, yes, positively, the order had been placed and gave me the exact date.

I immediately got Jean Swope on the line at Baker & Taylor and gave her the information. "It must have gotten lost," she insisted.

"No. There's a reason. And you better find it. But there's no time to waste now, I've got reviews coming out and I've got to get these books out to the stores. I'll get Duffy to do the order over again. At least I hope I will. And you better not lose it this time."

Thank God, and Jim Duffy, that he's a real person. "Please," I begged, "It's my whole career, Jim. We're a small company and we've bet everything we've got on this title. I don't know what happened and don't have time now to find out. The only solution is up to you."

"Okay, I'll do it over," he said.

I was somewhat relieved that both of the chain stores agreed to resend the orders to Baker & Taylor, but I still didn't know what, or who, was behind all this trouble. It had caused me to spend days and weeks chasing red herrings and fixing weird problems, and I knew it was affecting my performance—emotionally and physically. Yet I had no choice. Every fire which flared up had to be put out, or it would consume the whole book, and therefore, Affiliated Writers of America. All these weird occurrences strained nearly every personal relationship I had in the business.

Even after all that, aspect after aspect of business concerning the book went amuck; things that should flow normally and without ado landed into mysterious quagmires.

Next, it was Baker & Taylor dragging their feet to send purchase orders to cover the chain store orders. Weeks went by again. It didn't matter how often I called them, or that it was their fault that they lost the chainstore orders, nothing seemed to matter as the time flowed on and on, and the book sat in the warehouse of the printer, surrounded by orders and demand and yet unmoving, as if sentenced not to sell.

With reviews coming out and no books in the stores, I suddenly realized that this was no longer a matter of lost sales, it was a matter of *survival*. I went ahead and shipped a major portion of the books to Wyoming and warehoused them temporarily at the Yellow Freight terminal in Cheyenne, ready to be shipped at a moment's notice to Baker & Taylor. I knew the manager of the terminal well, and knew I could count on her. There wasn't much else I could do.

So I just dug in and waited, helpless and frustrated. Finally, finally, the magical purchase orders from Baker & Taylor came in, and with lightening speed, the truckloads of books went out to six Baker & Taylor warehouses all over the country. But there was still something strange because Jean Swope told me, "We got the Waldenbooks order, and another chainstore order, but there's no other demand. Zero besides the chains."

I'd never seen anything like it. The library market alone was thousands, we were the feature book review in *Library Journal*, and yet, zero?

Robin Moore was very concerned and calling nearly every day. "The guys in New York want to know when they can get books. The reviews are coming out. When can we start *selling*?"

I gave the same assurances I always had. And every day that something was supposed to happen, and I had reasonable expectation, which I passed along to Robin, it didn't happen, and I had egg on my face. This happened so often that Robin was panicked and beginning to lose faith. "You're the publisher! You're supposed to be able to avoid these problems."

"My God I'm trying!"

"You're not trying hard enough!"

"The hell I'm not. There's something wrong, Robin, I don't know who or why or what, but it's really weird. Now listen. The books have shipped to Baker & Taylor and they should be in the stores in ten days. We need to focus on publicity now to get people coming into the stores asking for books."

So we did. We flew to DC and provided a live press release and interview at the National Press Club and invited all the media in DC to attend. We did a National Public Radio interview, *nationwide*. In New York, there were more articles in the *New York Post* and on the wire through *Associated Press*. *Publishers Weekly* reviewed the book and that came out, along with numerous others. Robin and I worked publicity and ten days passed and just the thought of calling Baker & Taylor to check on the books in their warehouses made me cringe at this point. But I called them and asked anyway, just to be safe, just to follow up. Jean Swope checked the computer. Some of the books arrived and would go out to the chains, but then she said something that I was afraid I would hear: "No books in the New Jersey warehouse."

"But the New Jersey warehouse serves New York City! That's our biggest market, and you're telling me no books?"

The New Jersey shipment was lost. Gone. Literally didn't exist, even in the Yellow Freight computer system. Fuck!

It took another week to find the shipment. It turned up in a Baker & Taylor warehouse near Chicago. How the hell did this happen?

Then it took another week to get them shipped to New Jersey.

And another week to get them shipped to the bookstores in New York City.

All in all it wasted three weeks of my fucking time. Now, the special circumstances in life were upon me, and I used the "f" word to myself several times. What was happening was insane, and worse, I could sense that it wasn't over yet.

Finally, finally—I was told by Waldenbooks—books were in the stores in New York City. So I put the word out to Robin, the Duke, and everybody else I could think of. Go get 'em.

CHAPTER EIGHT
Title Unavailable

"They can't get the book."

"What?"

"They can't get the book." It was the Duke calling me in Wyoming from New Jersey. The FBI men that I had met personally were unable to get the book in New York.

"Bullshit! I told you, I told them, go to any Waldenbooks or Barnes & Noble store."

"We did. They did. They can't get the book. Nobody has it. And nobody can even order it."

"You mean they're sold out?"

"I don't know. I only know that the guys are pissed off because they can't get the book. And they want to know why you said it would be available in all the bookstores when it's not."

I was floored. "I don't know what's going on. But I'm going to find out. I'll be in New York tomorrow."

"Good. Now how about selling me some books so I can get them to the guys."

"Sure. Anything you want. How many do you want? Twenty?"

"For starters. Everybody wants the book, and it makes you look like a flake. I mean, you say you're a publisher and everything. Now you've lost your credibility."

"Jesus, how about five bucks a piece. That's a hundred bucks. I'll ship them to you today, and I'll pay the freight. You can sell them for twenty, you know."

"*Sell them*? No. Not now. I'm going to *give them away*."

I drank heavily on the plane to New York. The helpless feeling of knowing that something else was wrong—after all I'd been through—was too much at this point. I'd been a publisher for six years, and this had been so outrageous that I was just beside myself. And whoever was behind this was surely laughing loudly now—at their success—and my demise. It angered me to not know who was doing it. But it was real and still upon me. And the fact that I'd been discredited personally with the FBI in New York, and countless others of my personal and professional friends made me seethe with anger. And the whole thing was ghostlike. Nothing to grab. No one to question. No one to even *look* at, and I knew that even my own countenance had been destroyed. I looked like hell.

I was accustomed to greeting people with a smile, or at least a smile in my eyes. But now I couldn't hide the scorn and bitterness in my eyes and face. I was sad and overwhelmed. It was just another shitty day to me. A real fucking shitty day.

Remarkably, I guess because I was so depressed and worn out when I got to the Club in New York, I got a good night's sleep. Robin had arrived at the Club also and we were both up early.

We went together on a discovery trip down Fifth Avenue and entered the first Barnes & Noble store we saw and ask for *The Moscow Connection*. "And who's the author?" the clerk asked.

"Moore, Robin Moore," Robin said.

"It should be over here in the *m*'s. Nope. Don't have it. Would you like me to see if I can order it?"

"Yes," I said.

The clerk typed it into the computer and then said curtly, "We can't get it."

I was shocked. "Can't get it?"

"That's right," the clerk said and just abruptly walked off and approached another customer who appeared to need help.

"Wait a minute! Wait just a doggone minute. What do you mean *you can't get it*?" I asked and Robin's face looked ashen.

"Unavailable," he said impatiently, ignoring the magnitude of my concern and Robin's utter disbelief, turning once again to the other customer.

I wanted to slap this guy, but I collected my emotions and brought my voice to a deliberate and calculated tone. "I should tell you that I'm the publisher and that it certainly *is* available. Barnes & Noble bought the book nationally. So I know you can get it."

"It's not available on the computer."

"What database are you checking? Ingram?"

"Yes."

"Why don't you check the other wholesalers, like Baker & Taylor?"

"Because we're trained not to."

Those words stung so hard that they literally threw me into a daze. "You're kidding me. Baker & Taylor is the vendor of record, and you're not even going to look at their titles?"

"No, I'm not. Now, if you please...."

Robin looked at me, and I looked at Robin. It felt as if it were all happening under water, it felt as if we weren't even in the store, as if we weren't really hearing this, as if we were swirling in a huge current of water sucking us down to the Marianas Trench.

But hear it we did. All the other stores were the same. Sold out and couldn't get it. We didn't talk much as we walked, in fact I don't think we talked at all. I remember staring a lot at the grey, dirty sidewalk.

Back at The Metropolitan Club Robin set into drinking it off, and I didn't blame him. As much as I wanted to join him I fought the urge and got on the phone to Barnes & Noble. I got two of the buyers on, including Sessalee Hensley, one after the other, and explained that the book was sold out and needed to be reordered immediately, especially for the stores in New York City. The answer was a flat "No." It was as if I were talking underwater and blowing bubbles.

My next call went to the president of Barnes & Noble, Len Riggio—who surprisingly enough with everything else happening that day—took my call. I explained that the buyers had refused to reorder, and that we were all losing major sales because of the book being sold out and all the demand.

Len Riggio said, "Sold out! That's the best there is. You made money and we made money!"

"That's not the point. Nobody can get the book. We're losing sales."

"We're not going to reorder. It's done. It was a November book. This is December. A book gets three to six weeks with us. If it doesn't hit the best seller list, it's had its day."

I was incensed. The book had hardly hit the market. I explained that it never did have its day and sold out anyway because it was such a hot title. "It's not done. It's just getting started. The reviews are just coming out. And besides, there's another problem. Baker & Taylor is the vendor of record, and your clerks are saying the book is unavailable."

"That's right," he said.

This caught me totally off guard. "What do you mean?" I asked slowly.

"We train them to look only at the Ingram database."

"But that's not fair trade. What about all the other wholesalers, and books?"

"That's not my problem. We'll buy where we want. And we'll train our people the way we want. If you don't like it, take it up with them, or with the Federal Trade Commission."

The conversation went on for over half an hour and never got beyond these circles. Len Riggio would not override the decisions not to reorder, and it was certain that the lock on Barnes & Noble was—for that day and hour and moment in time—quite secure. "And you just got half an hour of my time," Riggio emphasized. "I don't just give that to anybody."

"I know. Thanks for taking my call," I said politely. After all, publishing *was* a polite industry. Yes. Yes indeed. And at the very least, he had been a gentleman.

I went back down and sat with Robin in The Met Club bar at his favorite table by the window and ordered myself a glass of chardonnay. We sat there for a moment in silence, and then I explained the conversations with the buyers and with Riggio. Robin had had a couple of drinks while I was gone, but he was still as sharp as a tack. A lot of people didn't understand that about him. He liked to drink but he could handle it, and I had never seen it take the sharp edge off his mind.

"So, if you don't have the Ingram account, you don't have distribution."

"I knew Ingram was powerful in the industry, but I didn't know the full extent of their power until today. I was trying to prove that I could do business without them. I've lost."

"It's okay, old pal. It happens to the best of us." Robin was sullen—accepting the fate of the young publisher who sat across from him—knowing that our losses would be massive. We both had a good deal of money invested, and he probably wondered if my firm could sustain the losses and survive.

"Isn't there something you can do?"

"No. It's impossible."

"Yes, but if you can't do business without them, then what are you going to do?"

"I don't know, Robin, I've spent the last twelve months putting all my eggs in the Baker & Taylor basket, trying to prove that a publisher could deliver a trade hardcover without Ingram. Now I've discovered with certainty that it can't be done. We didn't get a fair shot at the market, which was the one promise I made to you—*that we'd put it out into the market and let the market decide.* Well, without them, there's no market, to speak of."

"So eat crow and get that account. Or quit publishing. You can't fight the whole world."

"I don't want to fight the whole world! I don't want to fight anybody! I just want to publish books."

I went back in time and recapped the events, ending with, "You've seen how much work we've put into *The Moscow Connection*, and every other book we've both done in our careers, and we have to be able to count on the performance of the wholesaler."

Robin listened intently, already knowing much of what I'd said, nodding sympathetically on occasion as I spoke. When I finished, he simply said, "So what are you going to do?"

"I don't know, Robin. But I'm not giving up."

"You've got to have that account."

"I can't accept that. I can't accept what in my opinion amounts to collusion and a monopoly on something so important to free speech as book distribution. And that's what we have just seen in America. I just have to fight it."

"You can't change this industry on your own. You're only one guy, and a little one at that."

"Yeh, like Hemingway said, 'One man, alone, just ain't got no chance.' So what? I'm still me. I'm still in business."

"Yeh, but for how long? If you can't get distribution, it doesn't do any good to print books or even get reviews, for that matter."

"I know all of this, Robin. I told you, I don't know what I'm going to do. Right now I'm in shock with what I've seen and heard today." We talked some more but it turned into another circle of conversation, like the one with Riggio, a circle which there was no way out of unless the whole business of book distribution in America changed, which would require action by something the size of the Federal Trade Commission. That wasn't likely. The FTC was allowing every kind of merger imaginable—among publishers— among film producers—among news agencies—one had to wonder if we would have more than ten publishers and five producers in America by the end of the century. What good did it do for one author and one small publisher to discuss it, other than to humiliate their own senses of fair trade and American ideals?

"Stop!"

"Oh?"

"Stop. This is not productive. We are not beaten. We've lost money, yes, we've lost credibility, yes, especially me. You can always blame me. But I'm not giving up my principles, and I'm not giving up my career. I'm not giving in. I'm just going to do the best I can. And that means hoping we get more big news and hoping that people will at least buy the books we have at Baker & Taylor. We know there's some force behind this. We know it's censorship. We just can't prove it."

"Maybe we can," Robin said looking up from his glass.

"By what, trying to find out who Miss Hanson is?" I asked taking a long sip of wine myself.

"It's the government. I know it is. They're killing this book and this story. They've done it to me before." He went into another anecdote about *The Green Berets* and their efforts to stop that book.

"They've probably done it to me before, too. The book on Cuba." I briefly recapped how the bank seized my corporate assets within days of my calling the Pentagon for permission to print Dick Cheney's picture in the book. The bank seized my assets and I didn't even owe them any money yet—so I didn't dare use my line of credit. I ran

Affiliated Writers of America on $16.74 for two months until that book was printed. What the bank did was illegal in my opinion but the banking commission did absolutely nothing about it. It was also a mystery who paid Dick Cheney's tuition at Yale. My opinion was that they were connected, possibly even the same person. The banking commission wouldn't even disclose the ownership of the bank to me (it was a holding company and full of secrets). I survived it. I kept my spirit and kept working and then sued them later, and they settled the day before we were to take the deposition of the bank president. That was my first hardcover book. Right after the bank problem, the bindery refused to bind the book. Who got to them? So the printer helped me find another bindery and we shipped the signatures to Salt Lake City to get it done there. The printer stayed with me saying, "I don't like what my bank does to me either, so just pay me when you can. It's a great book and my pressmen and staff have been reading while it was in production. They all love it and want it to succeed." I was vindicated for my tenacity by the last sentence of *The New York Times Book Review* which said, *It is a precious story of spiritual survival and it will captivate anyone.*

"I don't want to sue anybody again," I said to Robin, "but I'm not giving up my principles either. I'll keep after the distribution and you just keep up the autographing and help me with the news. It's the best we can do."

It was set. No more counting losses. Fight fight fight. And that we did. We flew from New York City to Washington DC and even though Robin had become sicker than a dog—the stress and long hours got him down with the flu—Robin still went on the Jim Bohannon Show and the audience ordered record numbers of books through the 800 number. So we knew that if people heard about the book and could find it, they would buy it. We just had to get it into more news. My relationship with Jim was very strong. When Larry King quit his radio show (broadcast on the Mutual

Broadcasting Network of hundreds of radio stations nationwide) to take his present post at CNN, Jim Bohannon took over the position with radio, and the *Larry King Show* became the *Jim Bohannon Show*. Dinner was out because of his nocturnal life style and sleep schedule, but we used to meet for coffee or breakfast when he got off the show early in the morning. He had even offered the manuscript for his autobiography, which I read but didn't feel that it was a big enough book. Later, I wished I had published it and so did Jim. Another publisher picked it up and came up with the title *Almost Larry King*. Neither of us liked that title, especially Jim.

Robin went to work on an autographing tour in Massachusetts and Connecticut. I kept working the news.

Then there was a sudden change which really caught my attention: Connie Chung had been fired, and Gary Scurka quit CBS. I had Gary's home telephone number, and I called him. Gary confirmed it. He'd quit. And he'd quit to do the story about nukes on his own. CBS decided they had spent enough time and money on the story and were telling Gary to move on. Gary refused to stop working on the story.

"You mean you quit a top job at CBS to do this story?"

"That's right. I know I'm right, and I'm staking my whole career on it. I'm going to Lithuania with my own money and I'm going to get the story and film it myself."

"Are you going to do anything about our book and how it relates?"

"Your book is dead. And the pressure I'm getting from the government to drop this story is incredible. The FBI is harassing me, and at this point I believe they'll do anything to stop me, and you, and anybody else who wants to publicize the sale of nukes to terrorists."

"You know what, our book *is* dead. We've lost our asses on it. And I'm not even sure I know all the reasons. But I'm not giving up either. So what's the latest with your story?"

"The FBI is running me around in circles and trying to intimidate me."

"How, physically?"

"Yeh. I was in North Carolina covering a hearing and during a break two FBI agents barge in and flash their badges six inches from my face and shout, 'F—B—I!' in front of everyone there. And then they ask me to go up to their office with them and try pumping me for information."

"You're in the news. You're not doing anything wrong."

"I know it. And they know it. They're bluffing. But it works on some people, and I have to admit, it's scary, and it embarrassed me in front of those people. But you know what? I don't care. Because I've got the story, and I'm going to finish it, and I believe my source is innocent, and that the FBI framed him for reasons connected to the sale of Russian nukes. But I'll tell you this. Be ready for the same treatment if you keep trying to promote Robin's book."

"I don't believe they'd do anything that direct to me. I'm a publisher. And I don't think they'd want the bad publicity they'd get. Investigative journalism is one thing, but book publishing is another."

"Not really. It's all information—information they don't want Americans to know."

"Essentially, you're right. But in terms of what the book industry will tolerate, I think it would be major news if I were physically harassed over the subject matter of one of my books."

"I hope you're right. In your case, they may be more sophisticated in how they stop the book."

CHAPTER NINE
Blue Christmas

It was December 16th, Christmas was less than ten days away, and Robin was on tour in Connecticut autographing books and speaking in bookstores. It is the busiest and best time for the book industry, and we sell more books just before Christmas than any other time except maybe Father's Day. I was in Wyoming working late, sitting at my desk around dinnertime when the phone rang. It was Robin. He was hysterical.

"My God, they've short discounted my book!"

"What?"

"They've short discounted my book!"

"What in the world are you talking about?"

"My autographing in Torrington has been cancelled. The bookstore manager called me and ask if you were some kind of thief. 'My God,' he said, 'You can't expect a bookstore to pay nineteen dollars for a twenty dollar book.' Five percent!"

I was totally shocked. A bookstore manager had called me a thief, a 5 percent discount was unheard of, and I just sat there, stunned. I still couldn't believe it.

"Five percent?" I said in a very weak voice.

"They've short discounted the book to five percent. It should be at least 40 percent!" He was still hysterical. I had never heard him in such a state of mind.

"Who?!" I asked suddenly getting outraged myself.

"Baker & Taylor!!" He shouted even louder.

I had never seen him get hysterical over anything. He had balls as big as grapefruits and had the guts to write about anything from the mafia to Russian nukes. And for a moment I was getting outraged myself, but hearing this last, I calmed down.

"That's impossible," I said in a matter-of-fact tone. "We're in bed with Baker & Taylor. They are our best wholesaler. They are our vendor of record with the chains. They *are our pipeline* to all the bookstores in America. It's impossible."

Robin's voice now assumed a tone more grave than hysterical. "Jay—you better check this out. What I'm telling you is true. The manager at the bookstore cancelled my autographing because of this, and we've been had."

The brevity of the possibility began to sink in, and after everything I'd already been through on this book, I began to realize that the impossible could, in fact, be happening.

"I'll call their order line right now. They're still open, and I've got the number."

"You better. Call me back. It's insane. They've killed my book! You can't expect a bookstore to pay nineteen dollars for a twenty dollar book!"

"I don't! They're supposed to get 40 percent! I'll check it out."

I nervously dialed the 800 number for the order line. When the clerk answered I said, "I'd like to check availability on a title."

"Are you a bookstore, or a library? Who's calling?"

"A bookstore in Colorado."

"Go ahead."

"*Moscow Connection* by Robin Moore."

"Yes. It's available and in stock in hardcover. Twenty dollars."

"What's the discount?"

"Ew. Short discount. Five percent."

"What?"

"That's what it says."

"Are you sure?"

"Yes, let me check here, let's see, wow, we bought it at a 55 percent discount, it should be full discount, hmm, never seen this before. Must be something wrong with the publisher."

"I AM THE PUBLISHER!" I shouted and my blood was boiling. "What in the world is going on?" I asked incredulously.

"I don't know. I've never seen this."

"Well, there's nothing wrong with me, pal. I gave you trade discount, and you are supposed to pass that along to your customers."

"Well, you'll have to take that up elsewhere. I'm just an order clerk."

I was devastated. My only ally, my only chance to fight and win against that other wholesaler, had betrayed me. This was like hearing that your son had just been killed by a truck.

I called Robin. My voice was barely audible. "It's true," I said.

"What are we going to do?"

I don't know. I can't call anyone there until tomorrow."

"How could they do this?"

"I don't know. It's fraud. I had no idea. Gawd, no wonder the Waldenbooks order disappeared. God knows how many other orders dumped without us knowing it. No wonder there was no demand."

"I'm writing a letter to The Author's Guild. This is censorship. I just can't believe a company that size would think they could get away with this."

"Me either. But they did it. I'm going to get several bookstores to call and document this so I can prove it. Otherwise, I'm helpless until tomorrow morning. You know, Torrington is where we sold the serial rights to the newspaper. We could have sold hundreds of books there."

"I know, well, let's talk in the morning," Robin replied in a somber voice.

The next morning I sat bolt upright in my bed at first light, still searching my mind after a poor night's sleep. The news of the prior evening still had a dreamy, unreal quality to it, like it just couldn't be, like someone who'd lost their leg, and looking down the next day, wondered if it might have just been a bad dream.

Coffee and contemplation offered no clues. No solutions. No comfort. I knew I'd been had. I knew this day would just be a confirmation of the horror.

"Buying, Jean Swope," she answered, just like she always had, I'd worked with her for years.

"Hi Jean," I said. "It's Jay Fraser here with Affiliated Writers. We've got a major problem with *The Moscow Connection*."

"Really, what's that?"

"Pull it up on the computer and tell me what the discount is to bookstores."

"Oh no, it's on short discount. Someone must have hit the *N* key."

"It's only a 5 percent discount, isn't it."

"Yes."

"You know, I don't give you a 55 percent discount for you to only give 5 percent to your customers. That discount should be 40 percent!"

"I know. I'll see if I can get it changed."

"Great. But look at the sales we've lost. And I've been blamed for it and called a thief by at least one bookstore manager. I want the name of the person who did this."

"Oh, I can't give you that."

"Baloney. I want the name. Somebody's trying to stop this book, and I want to know who it is."

"Well, I can't tell you."

"Do you know?"

"Well, yes, the code of the person is right here in the computer, but I can't give it to you."

"I need to know. Like I know now why our chain store orders disappeared. Like I know why you kept saying 'no demand' even when we had national publicity and news. Like I know how this book has been killed in the market."

The conversation went into another circle with no end. She did say she'd changed the discount back to trade, but said she couldn't control it if someone else changed it back. And she wouldn't give the name of the person that did it, and without a name I was furious.

I called several others managers and vice-presidents of the company, but to no avail. I finally called Jim Ulsamer, the president, and explained the situation.

He seemed to be listening intently, and when I finished he said, "All right. I'll look into it and get back to you."

"Today?" I asked.

"Today," he assured.

When he called back it had been fairly quick. "You're right. The book was on short discount. But we can discount to our customers any way we want. We have lots of different discounts. You can't tell us what price to charge our customers. That would be a fair trade violation."

"Oh, baloney. I gave you a 55 percent discount, which is the trade wholesale discount, and you had a duty to give trade discount to the bookstores and libraries. I may not be able to tell you what your trade discount is, but I can expect that my book will be discounted with all your other trade books."

"Not necessarily. There are lots of other factors."

"Not in this case. You agreed to be vendor of record with the chain stores. Their computers automatically cancel any orders for short-discounted books. In our case, it was thousands of books."

Around and around it went again. Here came the circle. Then one final question. "I want the name of the person who did this."

The answer was no. That would remain a mystery. I decided to name her *Miss Hanson*.

So there I was, a week before Christmas, no sales to speak of, no books in the stores to speak of, and no real hope of publishing a best seller because now I was blocked by *two* major wholesalers. My hopes were dim even though the reviews had been generous and strongly positive. It was *acclaim*, not sales. And publishing companies can't run without sales. *The Moscow Connection* had been the lead book review in *The Library Journal*. It had been reviewed in *Publishers Weekly*. *Associated Press* did a national book review and put it out over the wire to practically every newspaper in America. And then, as if to top it off, on Christmas Day it was the lead book review in *The Boston Herald*. In January it was the lead book review in the *Los Angeles Times*. And no sales.

Robin contacted the Authors Guild in New York City and they sent a letter to Jim Ulsamer at Baker & Taylor. They sent me a copy as the publisher.

December 22, 1994
The Authors Guild, Inc.
Three Thirty West 42nd Street
New York, NY 10036

James Ulsamer
President
Baker & Taylor Books
Momence, Illinois

Dear Mr. Ulsamer:

I am writing to you on behalf of Authors Guild member Robin Moore, who wrote *The Moscow Connection, The French*

Connection, and many other books. The Authors Guild is the nation's oldest and largest organization of professional authors. It is not uncommon for us to intercede in the legal or business affairs of our members.

Mr. Moore contacted us because Baker & Taylor has refused to inform bookstores that the 42% discount on *The Moscow Connection* has been restored after an unexplained drop to 5% during the Christmas season. We are told that retailers all over the country stopped ordering the work due to the discount reduction, and many have told Mr. Moore that they will only order it again if Baker & Taylor notifies them that the 42% discount is back in effect.

If this is correct, then the financial damage to Mr. Moore may be substantial, and Baker & Taylor should take quick, effective action to tell bookstores of the proper discount. Baker & Taylor must, of course, relay to all of its stores now that the discount is 42%. To begin to repair the damages, you should also sponsor an ad in *Publishers Weekly* or *The New York Times Book Review.* Such action is the least Baker & Taylor can do in light of the loss in royalties Mr. Moore suffered during the holiday season, as well as the further injury he bears while bookstores are in the dark about this change. We were even told that the author had to cancel autographing sessions because retailers no longer had copies of the book in stock. Please inform the Authors Guild of what action you take in this regard.

Sincerely,

Paul Aiken
Assistant Director

The letter went largely unheeded. Baker & Taylor did send out a message printed on the back of the envelopes which they mail out each week to deliver their microfiche data to bookstores and libraries, but that was basically it. No ads in *The New York Times Book Review* and no ads in *Publishers Weekly*. Robin was very disappointed, and of course I was fit to be tied. And we soon learned that the Authors Guild letter carried no weight, in spite of all the big names on their letterhead. I called Paul Aiken and he basically informed me that the Guild had no legal fund and could not do anything more than send letters.

At this point it seemed inevitable that these events would take me and my company out of business. Except for one thing—the rest of the world—it would have. We sold numerous foreign rights on the book and that advance money saved the company and helped Robin also. It may have been censored in the USA, but not in other countries. The book was quickly translated into Japanese, German, Spanish, Dutch, and Korean. It was wonderful to see those contracts come in and sign them. Amazing how politics affect book publication.

Winter became bleak. Virtually none of the news writers or producers were interested in the story of the censorship of the book in the American market. Nobody could possibly believe that we have book censorship in America. We don't believe in that, right? Nobody could possibly believe that there could be a monopoly on book distribution in American bookstores, either, because publishing books is a noble endeavor, because we have a Federal Trade Commission, and antitrust laws, and we believe in a fair and free market. In theory. It couldn't happen any other way, right? Whenever I told this story to someone, or even part of it, people would drop their jaws for a moment, shocked, hardly able to even consider the idea that we may not have freedom of the press in America.

"Sure," I would say, "We're free to *print* anything we want. It's the distribution and news where the censorship occurs."

I had been hoping for a book review in *The New York Times* and now I needed it more than ever. I checked occasionally with the Book Review and had been told the book was *still under consideration*. This alone could have saved the book and pulled it back into the mainstream market. But time kept going by and my hopes diminished gradually, until it became apparent that even such a review couldn't help because of the blocking of the book in the market.

Suddenly, I read an article about Rebecca Sinkler retiring as book review editor. Why did she quit? I couldn't help but wonder if the review of the Moscow book had been stopped against her wishes. I couldn't know, and it would be pompous, perhaps, for me to even think that this one book could be that important to her, unless of course it was happening with other books too. And she did seem like the type of person whose ethics would rule in any major decision. So, another mystery appeared. Amidst the producers who quit on ethics, and the Connie Chung scandal, it seemed to fit a pattern.

I followed up with Christopher Harper at ABC's *20/20* to see if he might do a story of the killing of the book, and Chris had quit too! I got a number where I could reach him and called him.

"I'm teaching journalism for NYU now," he said.

"But why did you quit ABC?"

"I got tired of doing bullshit. I wanted to do real news and the administration wouldn't let me. I just got fed up. And quit."

"Good for you," but not good for me, I thought as I said it, "Good for you. I always thought you had integrity. But I really wish we could have done a story together."

"Me too. That was part of it. But there were many, many stories that were hands off. I just couldn't deal with it. I'm a journalist. At heart."

I wished him well, but I was also sad because it was another real journalist down the drain and out of production in the major news. The pattern was emerging, all right, reinforced again. I'm sure the network could find twenty producers for *20/20* who would do exactly as they were told with no qualms about *hands off*. It was bad news for America, and not good news for me because I wanted to continue publishing cutting-edge books and be on the leading edge of information. With such other, more powerful and more successful people quitting top jobs in New York, I knew the problem wasn't just me and my books, it was a problem with the news in general, and with book distribution, collusion, and monopolies which had broad implications for the whole nation.

So I wondered for the first time if the writing wasn't on the wall for my own career. Now, more than ever, I truly felt like the Hemingway man, *one man, alone, just ain't got no chance.* I began to feel I was in a daze. And feeling the plight of a Hemingway character set in Cuba, I prepared for my trip.

CHAPTER TEN
Censored in Cuba

Even though the Association of American Publishers (AAP) had been promised no censorship for the Americans by the Cuban authorities, I hadn't believed that for one second. How gullible could anyone be? One of the major proponents for the first American book exhibit in Cuba since 1959 was Rolland Allgrant, Vice President of Random House and a major member of AAP. I had a few discussions with Rollie prior to the March exhibit and I got the distinct impression that he was trying to block my participation in the exhibit and he was inferring that I joined AAP just to go on the trip as part of the group. It wasn't true, although this didn't surprise me. I had known Rollie previously because he called me shortly after *The New York Times* reviewed the book I published entitled *Leave Me My Spirit: An American's Story of Fourteen Years in Castro's Prisons* and expressed interest in acquiring paperback rights for Random House. We discussed it, but when I called him back in a day or so he wouldn't touch it. *I'm sorry I brought it up,* I said to myself, aggravated. It seemed somebody got to him and stopped that deal, too.

So he was less than helpful and even made things difficult for me to make the necessary arrangements for the trip. Nonetheless, I was very excited about joining AAP and now that I had an office in New York, and commuted there every other week, it was great timing. I had been thinking of joining AAP for years and had been recommended to contact Tim Hoops who used to be at the helm. It was hard for a company the size of mine to budget the money, and it was expensive. But I did it, and I was enthusiastic about joining and about seeing the mystery city and island which had been the setting of one of the best books I'd ever published. And I knew, and Rollie had to know, yes, we both knew that the book authored by a former CIA agent imprisoned in Cuba for fourteen years would never be allowed into Cuba by Castro.

I had said to Rollie over the phone, "No censorship? I don't believe that for one second. Castro is not going to let controversial books into Cuba."

Rollie was smug and talked down to me, not in the spirit of AAP. "We have assurances of no censorship."

I laughed. This liberal faction in America who wanted to believe such things about Cuba had actually convinced themselves within their own circles. And in some conversations, that statement would have flown. Not this one. "We'll see," I said, emphasizing the word *we*.

His smugness dried up a little after that, and I was certain that he did not want one of my books to put the acid test to the *assurances,* either. And Larry Lunt's story in *Leave Me My Spirit* would certainly do just that.

But why not put Cuban government assurances to the acid test? Why not? To cover up the fact that Cuban assurances are worthless? All this frou frou about going to Cuba and displaying books was great, but if the exhibit was going to be censored, what's the use? Are we, as American citizens, going to rubber stamp this treatment of books? I felt it was inevitable that someone was going to get egg on their face from this, and I really wanted to see it firsthand.

I also wish I could have put Rollie to the acid test and found out why he was hot for the rights to the Cuban book one day, and cold as ice the next. Wouldn't it be nice to know who he had talked with.

And it wasn't the first such strange hot-cold pressure the book *Leave Me My Spirit* had encountered. Long before I saw the manuscript, Jacqueline Kennedy Onassis wanted to publish the book as an editor for Doubleday (I had seen the handwritten letters from Jackie to Larry Lunt myself), and that too had been blocked somehow and never went through acquisition. Who had she called? Or who had found out and called her? The president of Doubleday at the time would probably have known. The reasons? Another enigma. Another Miss Hanson? One day I had met John Sargent, a former president of Doubleday before Bertlesman acquired it, while walking from the New York Athletic Club to The Met Club with Paul Pfeffer, the founder of the biggest international wholesale book company which had been acquired and later became Baker & Taylor International, a division of Baker & Taylor. Paul had expressed dismay to me about how Baker & Taylor had turned out, and that he was thinking of buying it back with a group of investors. After talking with me he was shocked, and said he was very glad we had talked. He told me that he would stop his efforts for buying the firm back. The facts killed that deal, and not many people knew what I had learned in such hard lessons. He wanted nothing to do with them. Paul and I had become very good friends and we met nearly every time I came to New York. I had been invited to join the Athletic Club and Paul had offered to sponsor me, but I couldn't afford it.

I had thought about broaching the subject of Jackie Kennedy, Lunt's manuscript, and her letter to John Sargent as we walked together on that Saint Patrick's Day toward Fifth Avenue where the great parade was in progress, but I had just been introduced to him by Paul Pfeffer and it seemed inappropriate at the moment. I later wished I had, as the opportunity never presented itself again.

Larry Lunt was at one time a very controversial man. His arrest in 1965 in Cuba and his incarceration through 1979 covered a very interesting time period (One true journalist—David Martin of *Newsweek* and later CBS—generated numerous news articles throughout the time and helped keep prospects of Larry's release alive). And there were numerous aspects of Larry's work for the CIA which, even at the time of my trip to Cuba—were still very sensitive. For one thing, I was told from a reliable source close to the case that Larry's handler in the CIA was also Lee Harvey Oswald's handler. Oswald, accused of assassinating JFK, and his alleged links to the CIA added frightening proportions to the trial of Larry Lunt—accused of trying to assassinate Fidel Castro. Later, there had been probes into assassination plots against Castro by the CIA, and Senator Frank Church had conducted Senate hearings on the matter. The day before he was to appear to testify, Larry Lunt's alleged handler was said to have committed suicide.

Was it? A reliable source informed me that Lunt's sister had been married to another CIA agent who was described as a sanctions enforcer (Two-Gun Teddy was his nickname). Suddenly he was found dead in front of their home in DC. He'd been hit by a car at night as he got out of his car in front of their house. A hit and run. If the handler's death had not been suicide, who had enforced the sanction? And then suddenly Two-Gun Teddy dead by hit and run. And so it went with everything related to Cuba, JFK, and Castro. Lots of dead people who may have known something. But Lunt was still alive.

There were very positive indications that Lunt would be released from prison just before the Church hearings but suddenly those negotiations got stalled. Lunt got out *after* the hearings were concluded and therefore could not be called to testify. When I published Lunt's book there were hundreds of people who came to me with information about the story. This is only part of it.

George Bush was then Director of the CIA, and Frank Carlucci was Deputy Director. From a reliable source, I discovered that Bush had tried to block President Carter's efforts to negotiate the release of Lunt, citing a Swiss Embassy Report on Lunt which was very negative. Carter didn't bow, and the release came through (1979). USA prisoners were released as part of the deal, and among them was Lolita Lebron (the Puerto Rican nationalist who had tried to assassinate Harry Truman at the Blair House and shot his body guard to death in the attempt, and who opened fire on the floor of the House of Representatives from the spectators' gallery with a machine gun injuring five Congressmen).

This was all front-page news—coast to coast—in 1979—I kept a file on it for a while—and Lunt's book must have had the hottest potential of the day—and must have also been the hottest political potato of the decade in terms of what could come out in his autobiography. The manuscript I got, however, contained nothing that I could see to deserve censorship. It was instead an excellent exposé and portrayal of Cuba and their prison system—of their wonderful, heroic people—and yet it was declined publication in the USA for ten years. I had been told that practically every major house in New York had rejected it. Yet when I published it (it was my first hardcover), it achieved tremendous acclaim with hundreds of major book reviews and news stories—all positive.

But the acclaim could not offset the sudden and tremendous, unexplainable (even today) occurrences which beset me and my small company—and which began—literally—the first day I called the Pentagon in 1990 and asked to speak to Secretary of Defense Dick Cheney (pictured in *Leave Me My Spirit*).

However, in spite of all this, to read the book would be to understand that lifting trade sanctions on Cuba would not help the majority of the Cuban people—it would only help the regime and those who work in it and support it. And further, that Cuba is not as it is portrayed in the USA press or in the USA books about the tiny island and its ruler. Lunt's story is hard to dispute because of the style of the writing and power of the writing, and also because Lunt had been there from 1955 to 1965 as a free man, and from 1965 to 1979 as a political prisoner. So why wouldn't a major house get behind such a book with sure success?

There's no way a major house would get behind the book. First, the government pressure not to. It's a partnership now between government and big business, and it was then too. But equally, every publishing house has what they call their "list." And their "list" is all the books they have already published on a given subject—in this case—Cuba—and their cacophony of books on Cuba ran the complete opposite direction from Lunt's story—supporting sympathy for Castro.

I had taken them all on by publishing the story and giving the book a chance in what I believed to be free and fair market. But I soon learned that those who opposed that book and others did not play fair. It was never face-to-face—it was—time and again— some secret trick. His book also had been short discounted without my knowledge. I'd been had from the beginning. Libraries and bookstores got cheated all over the country, and my sales were only a fraction of what they could have been. Even so, the book went into a second printing. It probably could have sold ten times as many copies as it did.

The differences between myself and Rolland Allgrant were not just over the exhibit, but also over Cuba itself. Rollie and most of the other members (not all) of AAP felt that trade sanctions against Cuba should be lifted, and that it would *help* the Cuban people. Perhaps, I reasoned, all of us going to Cuba together would offer some real experiences and observations which would serve as some good basis for discussions. After all, Castro's Cuba stood solid against the major-capital corporate giants. And maybe some of the editors and vice presidents who worked for giant publishing corporations themselves liked that. Who else could you say has stood up to the capitalists and their awesome power in America, on principle? I did, and look where it got me. But one thing seemed sure. They were not likely to align with me—the lone ranger from Wyoming and the publisher of Lunt's true story set in Cuba— regarding American foreign policy toward Cuba—the occurrence of book censorship in America—or the likelihood of it occurring at the book exhibit in Havana.

I packed over one hundred books to be sent to Miami, where they would be put into a container and sent then to Cuba. The books I sent were promised to be exhibited and then donated to the libraries in Havana. I intentionally packed Lunt's book in the middle of two separate boxes of books about Wyatt and Virgil Earp (Western peace officers). I then flew to the Bahamas where I spent one night in a hotel and the next day boarded a Cubana Airlines jet to Havana.

Seated next to me on the packed and overcrowded flight was Tom Francik (Managing Editor of *Reader's Digest* condensed books), and a Cuban stewardess came down the aisle pouring rum and orange juice for passengers who wanted a drink. When she got to our seats, Tom said yes, he'd like a glass and I said no thanks. Then Tom said, "Jay, you've got to taste the rum. It's the best in the world."

"I don't drink rum, I don't like it," I said.

"This is not ordinary rum. You've never tasted anything like it."

So I took a glass and tried it. It was seven-year Havana Club rum; it was black and very dark, even when mixed with a dash of orange juice. It was absolutely a phenomenal taste. It would become my drink of choice in the States, even today, if I could get it. It was my first taste on the trip of how fine Cuban products can be.

Stepping onto the tarmac and walking into José Martí Airport felt strange as a citizen of the USA—and as a publisher of a book which—however politely—was very anti-Castro. I would never have gone there alone without the AAP and the safety of numbers. I had decided to only go places with others or in groups—at least accompanied by one other executive from the AAP group. By myself, I just felt too vulnerable that something weird could just *happen*.

Going through customs took hours. Some of the Americans with me were detained, thoroughly searched, and treated a bit roughly. Those members were activists with human rights groups. Me, I was not harassed in the least, although some of the security personnel gave me looks that indicated they would have liked to bother me. I was cautious, very formal, and very polite. I knew Cuban intelligence was clever. And I knew I couldn't know all their plans or motives concerning my treatment there. Frankly, it was scary.

Checking into the Hotel Nationale was somewhat surreal and strange. There was an oddity to all of it—it was such an oddity that I couldn't place it. The Cubans had a strange regard for Americans, which was definitely part of it. As I spent more time there, it seemed there were two distinct categories of Cubans: those in support of the regime, and those on the outs with it. The ones in support wanted as little contact as possible with me—they were very standoffish. The ones on the outs—they wanted to know us. In any case, there was a strained aspect to it, heavy, like *who might be watching or listening?*

The next day there were several large meetings with Cuban officials and AAP officials presiding jointly in various rooms of the capitol building, which had been designed after and looked very similar to the White House—tall columns, marble floors, and marble walls. The exhibit was to be conducted in the capitol building.

I sat through some of the meetings and they seemed a bunch of pomp and grandiloquence—a veil for subtle debates on propaganda. So I took a break and wandered through the halls and other rooms in the building, observing the exquisite artwork, and watching the displays for the exhibit being erected and boxes of books carted in and opened and placed on the newly installed shelves and stands. Carton after carton came in and the crews put them out for display. It was an exciting thought that Cubans would be able to come in freely and see and touch the American books for the first time in over thirty years—and hopefully—read them in the libraries later— or even read parts of them here, on the spot.

I was there for quite a while, and as the day went on—I smoked an occasional Cuban cigar—watching—smoking—all of the books I sent hit the shelves but one: Lunt's book about Cuba. It was nowhere to be seen. When I saw the crews packing up their things to leave, I asked if there were any more books coming. The answer—in both English and Spanish—was, "No, that's all of the books."

The exhibit was scheduled to open the next day at noon with an official ribbon-cutting ceremony, but I knew the day before that my book about Cuba had been censored out. I didn't like it, and I mentioned it later to the international consultant AAP had hired to run and manage the exhibit. He was surprised, and didn't like it himself.

The next thing I knew—and it didn't take very long—a camera crew converged on me. It was Terence Smith, *CBS News*, Washington DC, in Havana and covering the exhibit. He held out a microphone and in the white light of it all and camera running, he said, "Mr. Fraser?"

"Yes," I said.

"Terence Smith, *CBS News*, Washington. I understand one of your books has been censored from the exhibit."

I was surprised, but I decided to be diplomatic in hopes that something good could come from the news about it, also realizing I was standing in a communist country. I said, "It appears to be the case. The Cubans have been notified and claim that they are looking for the book. I know the book got here because it was packed with Wyatt Earp books in the same box, and those books are here."

"But the book is not on display."

"No, it's not." I went on about the title and the significance of the book and about the promises of no censorship and then concluded, "I'm an American. We don't believe in censorship in America. So let's see what happens tomorrow. Let's see if they *find* the book and get it on display." What I was also thinking about was the book censorship we have in our own country, but I didn't go into that. That was another, much bigger fight.

The next day, of course, there was no book. And that day I attended a meeting set to discuss the matter. In attendance was an AAP representative and several Cuban government officials in charge of the exhibit. I had seen some of them speaking at the meetings the day before—and I found out shortly after the meeting that one of them was a high-ranking Cuban intelligence official. In the ensuing discussion they repeatedly but not too wholeheartedly claimed the book was simply nowhere to be found. I rolled my eyes at them and smiled, and the Cuban intelligence official looked at me directly and said, "Oh—well—perhaps another American will come to Cuba—to spy for the CIA—and will get caught—and go to prison—and get out—and write another book." Weren't they clever?

The next time the camera crew converged on me—and it wasn't long—I let them have the whole story, said exactly what happened, and said that I didn't like it.

The story aired nationally on *CBS Evening News* and then aired again on *CBS Sunday Morning* special edition. Good. The news covered book censorship in Cuba. But would they cover a story about book censorship in the USA, *in their own nest, in the so-called free land?* This last, I have yet to discover. This book will be the acid test for that.

The next day was the opening day of the exhibit and there was talk about calling it off because of censorship and the broken promise by the Cuban officials. But of course, the Rollie Allgrants were so proud of the exhibit that a little censorship shouldn't get in the way of them displaying *their* books. After all, at least there *was* an exhibit. To me, a free press was the most important single aspect of publishing, but to them, other agendas were more important, like hobnobbing with Cuban officials. I could see the mockery in the face of the Cuban officials as they dealt with the Americans. The Cuban officials knew, of course, the truth about the so-called Cuban public attending the book exhibit. They were laughing at all of the Americans with their eyes. And I could sense something amiss. I just looked right through them. It was only by accident that I discovered the truth about who could and could not attend the exhibit.

Later, I had gone out of the building for a walk by myself (deciding that in broad daylight downtown and close to the exhibit, it would be all right). It was a very warm day in March and I walked along the sidewalks and watched the images (trite now because Hollywood loves to exploit them) of the old American cars puffing blue smoke from worn-out piston rings, rolling along slowly on bald tires, dodging bicycles, against a backdrop of dilapidated buildings of Spanish architecture with peeling paint, and civilians walking the streets with uncanny gaits wearing tattered, worn-out clothes.

As I walked the sidewalk, several times, Cubans would approach me and it would go like this. Upon seeing me closer one would stop and ask, "Are you from the States?" in good English.

"Yes," I would reply, welcoming their greeting.

Then we would both stop walking and face each other and suddenly they would get a flash of fear or discomfort and their eyes would go flat and they would ask, "Why are you here? It isn't allowed you know."

Hoping to put them at ease, I would say, "It's okay, I'm here for a book exhibit. I'm here with permission."

The discomfort would go away and a bright countenance would reappear on their faces, and then suddenly the discomfort would return, and they would glance around quickly and then say something like, "Oh, then you're with the government."

"No. I'm here to exhibit books as an American publisher. Haven't you heard about the exhibit?"

"No. Nothing. But can I walk with you and practice my English? How am I doing, can you understand me?"

"Yes, of course, you're speaking very good English. I'm surprised."

They would then blush, and the fear would be gone, but their eyes would still glance around a bit and I knew about that. My eyes too, would glance around to see who was watching— it was instinct. You could feel it. And whenever at a glance I would catch an image of a Cuban policeman in those dark-blue uniforms with black belts and tall, black boots and a red stripe on one arm at the shoulder and a round, white patch on the other sleeve, within a second I would look back and they had vanished from sight. I caught onto this and tried to photograph them but they were too good at disappearing. Only rarely did I get them on film before they could duck behind a lamppost or the edge of some building. I think I only got one on film during my whole week in Havana.

As I walked with several Cubans who wanted to talk with me and practice their English and learn about the States, I noticed how those Cubans with me regarded other passersby on the street: some without reaction, but some with that instant fear in their eyes and sudden silence. They seemed to know who was part of the regime and who wasn't—at a glance. People who have never visited a communist country may not understand this, but there are only two types of people: the oppressors and the oppressed. The former became easier for me to recognize, usually somewhat overweight and arrogant and seemingly comfortable in their surroundings—if not in outright *control* of their surroundings. In contrast—and there was usually quite a contrast—the latter were usually thin if not malnourished, submissive in their demeanor, and *unsure* of their social surroundings. One glance from the former to the latter could abruptly end a conversation or an encounter, literally with the latter stopping mid-sentence and turning on their heels in a different direction—walking away sullenly.

To experience this several times struck me with some brevity. I walked the entire area in downtown Havana where the capitol building was, and nobody I asked had even heard of the exhibit.

So I decided to invite someone. I met another Cuban who spoke English with me and walked with me, practicing his English, and as we walked I invited him to come with me to the exhibit.

"Oh, no," he said and fear came into his eyes and he stopped walking.

"Yes. Yes. It's okay. It's open to the public. Anyone can come and see the books."

"American books? Oh, no. It's not so."

"Yes it is. Come with me now. Come on, you come in with me and I'll show you."

He came along but was very nervous even though I continually assured him it was okay as we mounted the tall steps to the entrance of the capitol. And all of a sudden swarms of police came out of nowhere—appearing on the sidewalks and on the grounds of the building—to watch me escort this Cuban citizen up the steps toward the doors which led to the exhibit. The Cuban noticed it too, and all the police were looking at the two of us, and the Cuban suddenly stopped on one of the steps.

"It's all right," I assured him again, "You're with me." I looked at him and it was with the greatest of courage that he continued with me up those steps.

So up we went and when we got to the doors there were guards who were dressed like clerks working the door—but they were *guards*—they looked at me and smiled and gestured me on into the exhibit, and as I moved forward I quickly looked back and they had made eye contact with the Cuban and glared at him and shook their heads and pointed back down the stairs like you would order a bad dog off a couch.

The Cuban turned back quickly and headed down the steps but I had seen it all; and I caught up to him and took him by the hand and tried once again to get him in, and the guards stood fast and spoke Spanish so fast I couldn't follow it, and the Cuban took off once again down the stairs—even more quickly this time—as fast as he could walk, and the police lingered on the sidewalks all around him, waiting, so they could follow him, so they could do their stuff to him as soon as he was out of my sight.

Oh, yeah, some fucking exhibit. Open to the public my ass. Now I'd gotten some poor Cuban off the streets into trouble. It was a lie. The whole exhibit was a lie. I felt like shit for getting someone innocent into trouble. I was pissed, real pissed off.

I went straight to Nick Veliotes and other AAP officials and told them the exhibit was a hoax and that it was staged, and that all the people in there were planted by the government. Nick *almost* refused to give a speech and cut the ribbon for the grand ceremony, but then he went ahead and did it anyway. What bullshit.

So I watched it all from the midst of a fake crowd of regalia and flags and cheers and all that stuff and was sickened by the continuation of the hoax and by the fact that the AAP members were turning a blind eye to it so they could aggrandize the first, wonderful, American book exhibit since 1959, with no censorship and open to the public. Puke.

Now that the exhibit had proven to be fakaloo right down to even the people the government brought in to be the fake public, it bored me. I felt defeated. I had tried to fight for free speech and free attendance, and I felt like the only one doing so (except for that brave reporter Terry Smith with CBS). So I decided to see what I could of Cuba, provided that I could interest a few other AAP members in doing the same. I still didn't want to go anywhere alone, not for fear of the Cuban people, but for reasonable caution against possible government action.

I found several people who wanted to see Hemingway's house on the hill which overlooked Havana where he used to live and write, so we all went in what must have been a 1959 Dodge which was in use as a cab. Its faded blue paint and matching blue smoke mixed with the hot, humid, afternoon Havana air as we drove the streets and the car laboriously climbed up the steep grades which led to the old house which had been elegantly preserved as a museum and monument to the great writer.

Upon arrival, there was a tour guide who led our group into the house, and I quickly became bored. I never had liked to be led around by tour guides, I liked to explore on my own and look at what I want to look at. So I walked off—out of the house—and onto the meticulously kept grounds, where I wandered through the various gardens which Hemingway had kept there. Walking around, I noticed Terry Smith. We stood together and talked a bit, and then I went back up to the house and stood in the back yard.

I was met quickly and briskly by a female guard of the house who saw my camera and said to me in good English, "No pictures allowed. We have photographs you can buy." Her voice was very authoritarian—one of the *oppressors*—I thought to myself—and I simply nodded and shrugged in submission. I moved away from her and walked over to a small wall around the patio where I sat down feeling, and probably looking, once again, defeated.

Then, another female guard for the premises saw me sitting there and approached me. The young lady looked around in all directions, and seeing that nobody was watching her, she motioned for me to stand up, which I did.

"You're the publisher, aren't you."

I wanted to ask *which publisher* but I was stunned. She seemed to know who I was, about the trouble at the exhibit, and about Lunt's book. So I guess that's how I was known, as the *publisher*, the American publisher. I was about to say something but before I could speak she put her finger to her lips, and I accordingly was silent but I cocked my head as if to ask why. She answered me with another silent gesture with her hand—this time—one swipe down from her chin as if stroking a beard.

I got it. Castro. Electronic surveillance. The whole place was bugged. She couldn't, or wouldn't, dare to say his name. I'll bet nobody did in Havana. The gesture of "the bearded one" had been a bold one, and I knew not to speak, and she led me around on a little walk and to a round addition to the house. We went up some obscure, winding stairs and when we got to the top we entered a large, round room—a room nobody was allowed to enter—it was the room where Hemingway sat to write, and his desk was still there, kept perfectly as I presumed it had been decades ago, complete with the lion's skin and head under the desk and facing out toward the room from where Hemingway's feet would have been placed on the hair of the lion skin. The chair, also, sat on the lion's fur and the desk was but a four-legged table with an old, black typewriter in the center. To the right in somewhat an area all to itself stood a large telescope on a tripod, and there were large windows on the blue walls, framed in white trim, through which one could look down and see the hills of the countryside and in the distance below—

Havana. There was a bookcase but I did not venture that close to the desk to see what books might have been on the shelves, rather, I was drawn to a glass case at eye level which enclosed several pictures and trophies for fishing, among them, one large photograph of Hemingway and Castro smiling together, and Hemingway holding the giant fishing trophy which sat in real life in the case in front of the picture and in front of me.

It was the only photograph of Castro I was to see in Cuba, and now the element of fear of his regime on the island took new dimensions, as people were afraid to even say his name. El Maximo leader had exacted el maximo fear from his people. I stood in the room in awe and held my camera up and gave the guard an asking look. There was a silence as she thought and the fear set into her, but then she nodded a tiny little nod of okay. Gawd what courage these Cubans had! I took slide film shots and quickly we were out of there and down the tiny, winding stairway. I glowed and whispered thanks and pressed her warm hand. I felt alive again and more resolved than ever to fight for free speech and free press and freedom.

Once back in the sight of others, she resumed her brisk, uniformed guard demeanor, especially toward me, and she showed no recognition or acknowledgement of my occasional, nonchalant glance as I walked through several rooms in the house set up for the tour by the Cubans and waited for the others to finish the tour. As usual, I became impatient, and went outside to stand near the blue 1959 Dodge and wait for everyone there. Once again, I saw Terry Smith, this time with his camera crew, and I took a few pictures and someone took a picture of the two of us standing together.

That night there was to be a meeting with several Cuban writers and the meeting was at a certain house in Havana. I attended, and as I rode in the cab I got a very strange feeling about it. The streets were dark and I lost my sense of direction.

When I saw the house, it really struck me as odd and ominous. The street—like the others— was very dark, and the courtyard of the house—the entire house for that matter—was surrounded by a thick, iron-barred wall, and we entered through very heavy, medieval-looking iron gates which hung from the thick iron wall on each side. There were lights in the courtyard—just enough light to see the Cuban "hosts" who were there to receive the AAP members and other Cubans. Upon entering, I strode about the courtyard in the dim light and hung around outside rather than go inside the large house with the others. I guess I just wanted to see what the deal was with those big iron gates. They really made me uncomfortable, and I didn't like the feeling of it all, and then again—just like at the capitol building—I saw several Cubans turned away from the meeting.

Suddenly, Terry Smith and his camera crew appeared and entered through the gate. They were instantly and abruptly confronted and instructed to leave immediately in very harsh tones. Terry tried to stand his ground and argued and explained that he was with CBS and here from Washington for the news.

Just as suddenly, several very-large-bodied men literally came out of nowhere—like from the bushes or something from the dark—and grabbed Terry by the arms and literally picked him up and manhandled him and dragged him out past that big gate and shoved him onto the sidewalk. Terry was a pretty good sized man, but these men were huge and after throwing him out and his camera after him, they closed the gate and locked it with a giant lock on a very thick chain. I'd had a bad feeling about this place all along, but now I really didn't like it. These men were like thugs. They wore very plain clothing, not uniforms, and they gave me creepy looks as I moved a little closer to the gate to see the medieval-looking lock, which I instantly realized not only locked Terry Smith out, but myself and the others in.

I felt jailed and Terry Smith must have perceived it, because he assembled the camera crew right outside the gate in spite of the thugs and shot footage of me standing there looking out at his crew through the bars of the gate, which aired on the evening CBS national news in the States. It made me appear as if I were in jail in Havana.

After that was over, I went inside the house and joined the others for the meeting. Once again, it seemed set up by the Cuban government. Parts of it did get heated, though, like when Wendy Wolf (AAP member and chair of the Freedom to Publish Committee) spoke out against censoring certain Cuban writers, and how some were in jail for their writing. I decided not to speak out at the meeting, feeling that there weren't any Cubans there that it would matter to anyway.

The next day, I decided to meet with a couple of Cuban publishers who, of course, were all arms of the government. My main question—handled through translators—went to the top editor of one of the companies. "What Cuban writer is there that I might publish in the States who writes about the land of Cuba?"

There was laughter and the response. "We Cubans don't share this love affair with the land like you Americans. Cubans are coming into the cities like Havana in waves, and we can't keep them in the rural areas. No, there is no such writer in Cuba."

After seven days in Havana, I had to agree. There were no such writers, at least, no such writers with the approval of the government. And those were the only ones I would ever get to meet. It made me think of the tour through Old Havana when I stood near the banks of the harbor and looked across at the walls to La Cabaña Prison on the other side. The tour guide had pointed it out and declared, "There are the walls to the old Spanish prison, La Cabaña, but of course it's shut down today. There haven't been any prisoners there for years." I just shook my head. I was probably the only one who knew every

detail of the prison as Larry Lunt had described it in his book, and
that there were probably five times as many prisoners in there right
then than the Spanish had designed the prison to handle.

The Cubans had been great at handing out propaganda to the
AAP members whom they were sure wouldn't know the difference.
At least one member knew the difference, and all the lies were
beginning to bore me, rather than incite me. Perhaps that's what
had happened to the Cuban people. So many lies that it's boring.
Would this happen, or has it already, in the United States?

As I left Cuba, I cherished the numerous rolls of slide and print
film I had taken and relished the thought of writing about the trip
and sharing the photos and slides. Guarding them carefully, I put
all the rolls of film into my front pockets as I went through customs
at José Martí airport. And the Cubans waved me through without
any ado.

My flight was back to the Bahamas, where I spent two days
before returning to the States and flying home to Wyoming. I had
carried my film in my pockets through customs in Nassau, and
once through that, and officially in the States, I trusted that the film
would be safe in my bags. So I took it out of my bulging suit-pants
pockets and placed it in a pouch in one of my bags which I checked
with United Airlines.

Wrong move. That bag disappeared for a week. And United was
extremely rude about it even though I was a premier status flier.
When I finally did get my bag, half the film was gone. Somebody
took half the film out of my luggage, another Miss Hanson? Which
half? It was more than half, actually. Quite a bit of the best. Could
never be replaced. So much for privacy and personal rights in
America. And United Airlines? They were scumbags about it.

I was back in New York City in the next several days and at our
next AAP Freedom to Publish Committee meeting (I was on the

committee), it was practically unanimous that AAP should lobby Congress and the president to get the trade sanctions against Cuba lifted. Although I knew privately that several people in the room disagreed, not a single one of them was willing to speak out against the majority in the room. It was a people thing. A bandwagon effect. But I spoke out, and directed my comments to Rollie Allgrant part of the time. "I think we should encourage the government to make them tighter, not lift them. The only people who will benefit from trade with the United States are the oppressors, the members of the Castro regime. The common people are not going to get anything out of it. Lifting sanctions will only help those in power—to stay in power—and prolong the agony of the victims of the regime." Of course, those words did not change the thinking of those in power in the room, but they did have effects because the letter that was to be written could not claim "unanimous" because I had been a vocal dissenter, but it could claim "majority."

It seemed ironic that the members of AAP would side with Castro's regime of over thirty years of dictatorship, ignore the censorship of their book exhibit there (and tolerate the lies that there wouldn't be), and send such a letter to US government officials. But then, I figured that as prominent leaders of major New York publishing houses, they knew the evils of capitalism and the harm that giant corporations were doing to the world. And Castro definitely stood defiant against the giant corporations. Even so, the plight of a small publisher who had been censored in the United States was of no interest to them whatsoever. The book applecart must go on. It's just a small company. One book about nuclear terrorism. The first novel about it. It can't happen here. So don't bother looking at the cart upon which the big apples in the Big Apple ride on so comfortably.

Here you see a policeman walking and a citizen on the sidewalk glancing at him. The police are feared in Cuba; it is very much a totalitarian state. Looks of disdain or fear were common toward the police, although the police did their best to stay out of my view. Sometimes I would try to take their picture and by the time I could raise my camera they had cleverly stepped behind a lamppost or into an alley or entryway. They seemed very practiced at not being seen.

I was standing in front of a police station with their cars to my right. In the far distance you can see La Cabaña—one of Cuba's oldest and most feared prisons. The walls are 12-feet thick; the moats are 30-feet deep and 40-feet wide. Cuban officials claim it is no longer used to house prisoners, however it is believed otherwise.

Rolland Allgrant (not pictured in this polaroid snapshot), Teresa Zampino, and I had become friends on the trip and one of our best times was going to the Tropicana together where we watched one of the greatest dance shows in the world. Rollie and I indulged ourselves in Montecristo number five cigars and remained friends after the trip despite our differences.

Six large cannons once protected the entrance to Havana Harbor from invasions or pirates. I wondered about the days of the tall ships and slave trade of the past.

Many such garrisons, cannons, and large, stone buildings were prominent throughout Havana—so much history remained intact and visible. Even the harbor itself could remind a person of the African slave trade between the US and Cuba that once flourished. *La Amistad*, a slave-trading ship named "the friend," sailed from Havana to the US in 1839. The story of the ship's mutiny en route to the US became a popular movie in 1997.

Men sitting idle were a common sight. I often wondered if they had some duty or mission. Some did not smile at me.

The Partigas cigar factory is in the middle of Havana near the capital. The rumor was Arnold Schwarzenegger had visited and had been given some cigars. I had to buy mine.

Buses were packed to the maximum with passengers since few could afford autos. There were usually long lines and very large crowds at bus stops.

There is a tunnel underneath the harbor and hundreds—if not a thousand or more—waited to cross on bicycles. Russian supplies of gasoline had collapsed with the former Soviet Union.

I could only wonder at the history of the past as I saw the military castles.

Even these centuries-old canons probably protected against invasion from the nearby harbor. Barely visible in the background skyline on top of the hill is La Cabaña Prison.

Dilapidated buildings abounded. Glass and paint were in very short supply. People in apartment buildings often stared out through big openings, and blankets hung in place of glass.

Some buildings gave the impression of a war zone. Note the 1950s, red car in the lower right-hand corner. Most of the cars had worn-out engines and smoked a lot.

There seemed to be some remodeling going on in the city, but this was the only place I actually saw it, however, and some of the "entrepreneurship" seemed staged for us to be paraded through it so we would think there was some free enterprise on the streets. There were workmen, such as these pictured on the scaffold, but I didn't see any of them actually doing any work.

Same street, lots of people walking, nobody buying. The old Spanish architecture which accented nearly every vista of the city spoke of a different, perhaps prosperous past.

This was the only such sign that I saw in Cuba. Taking a taxi to Hemingway's house probably took me outside my expected area of visitation.

The driveway which leads to Hemingway's house was surrounded by lush gardens and well-kept grounds. There were no signs or advertisements whatsoever at the entrance, on the grounds, or on the street.

These are the views that Hemingway would have looked at with the telescope on the tripod (pictured later) which stood in the room next to the desk where he wrote.

On the front porch of Hemingway's house, I stand with Terence Smith (pictured left), CBS News, Washington Bureau.

The CBS camera crew, which filmed me on numerous locations following the story of my censorship at the book exhibit, was also at Hemingway's house with Terence Smith.

The photo on the left with Castro and Hemingway displaying their fishing trophies was the only picture of Castro I saw.

Hemingway's desk where he put his bare feet on the lion's skin as he wrote was in the highest room in the house. Visitors were not allowed into the room and probably didn't even know it existed. However, one of the guards motioned for me to follow her up the secluded, spiral staircase to the room. I felt very honored.

Three of my titles appeared in this display with other American books—
The Moscow Connection, People of the Whistling Waters, and *Blue Sky, Night
Thunder.* The 1990 autobiography of the CIA agent in Cuba during the
missile crisis of the 1960s mysteriously disappeared from a box of other
books that *did* make it to the exhibit.

We were told the exhibit was open to the public, yet when I invited people I met on the street and tried to bring them into the building with me, guards appeared to harshly refuse them entrance. I felt stupid for believing the exhibit was actually open to the public and hoped no harm came to them out of my invitation. All the guests at our exhibit were staged government visitors—not the public.

We were taken on a tour to see a Cuban book exhibit on the sidewalk of a street—perhaps just to let us know that there are actually books available for sale in Cuba.

Although the Cuban beaches were absolutely beautiful, they were practically vacant.

There were a few clusters of people, however, gathered around a table or two seemingly enjoying the day outdoors.

A man stands in the shade of a palm tree somewhat hopelessly—trying to rent out a horse to ride—not too many customers.

Teresa Zampino, the international sales manager from Bantam, Doubleday, Dell, watches a very low-flying aircraft which made several threatening passes as low as 50-feet and once flew right at my head.

Cuban-born Teresa Zampino had been taken to the USA at age three, and we looked for and found the house in Havana where she had been born.

A seventeen year old Cuban waves to me and stands for this picture. She was the only one swimming in the ocean that day, except for me, and I taught her how to body surf. A man standing on the beach watching her was--I thought--her father. But he was a Mexican Airlines pilot hoping to take her with him as he left the beach. Teresa Zampino and I gave her a ride to her home in Havana in the cab with us, instead.

CHAPTER ELEVEN
Librarians and Politicians

The months to follow began a downward spiral which seemed inevitable. The 1995 winter in Wyoming continued through April and May and even the summer was so cold that it snowed on the Fourth of July. I was thrown into a period of analysis and retreat. My company, for which sales had either doubled or tripled each year, was now at a standstill. And worst of all, among the several authors and books which I had opportunity to publish, I could no longer make the promise in good faith that I had distribution in the market. A dubious discounting situation with Baker & Taylor coupled with an even more dubious iron gate with another major wholesaler was the equivalent of a naval blockade. With no gunships of my own (big-gun lawyers) and very limited supplies (no money), I could only sit and wonder. How could I fight? I thought about David and Goliath. If there would have been two Goliaths, David would have lost. I certainly couldn't fight both wholesalers at the same time. Robin Moore and other authors offered support, however, it really came down to the issues of distribution. The Authors Guild had no teeth and no will to dive in, and at AAP, nobody seemed to care. There was lots of concern everywhere else in the world about gay writers and their rights, political writers and their rights, but not even a smidgeon of interest in a case of real censorship in the United States. What now?

Robin Moore had written a new book about supernatural forces on an island in the Atlantic off the coast of Massachusetts, but I didn't feel that my publishing company was positioned well enough to publish it. Still, however, Robin wanted me to edit the book, and I agreed to do it.

We went to the island for the duration of the task. Cuttyhunk Island (the end of the Elizabeth Island chain past Martha's Vineyard on the Atlantic coast) had some of the best striped bass fishing on the east coast, and Robin had a house there near the edge of the water where the cliffs stood out over the beach, and there was a little fishing dock at the bottom of the cliffs where we could go to try to catch the stripers.

The very night we finished editing the book, there was a moon tide (higher than usual), and as if the forces themselves had gotten me, my foot slipped as I jumped onto the dock that evening and my shin landed squarely on the edge of the dock. It shattered the bone in my shin and I collapsed on the dock. The pain was so intense that it took the wind out of me.

Barely able to breathe, I called out to Robin on the shore. "Robin! I think I just broke my leg!"

"What?" Robin replied as he looked and saw me sprawled out on the dock. I moved my leg and saw it swivel between the knee and the ankle and the bones moved around like they were loose in a sack of skin.

When I saw that (and felt it!), I called out to Robin again. "I know I broke my leg!" I exclaimed, looking up the tall cliff that stood between us and the house and help. The brevity sank in fast and the pain was simply wild.

"Oh my God. What are we going to do?" Robin replied, also apparently realizing the remoteness of the island and lack of any medical services whatsoever.

"Help me get off this dock," I said, realizing I had to take control and also feeling the shock setting into my body already, and the spray of the splashing salt-waves didn't help the clamminess creeping into my now-sweating skin. I pulled myself up with the use of the rail on the dock and got onto my one good leg, and then hopped on it to the edge of the dock where it was a two-foot leap down to the rocky shoreline. I would have to jump and land on one foot on the wet rocks and in water because of the full moon and higher than normal water.

My instructions to Robin were spoken in between breaths of air, I still couldn't catch my breath because of the pain. "Come over here—and stand—right here—I'm going—to jump—on one foot—and—I'll put my—arms around you—and—hang onto your neck—and—are you ready?—and here we go—on three—one—two—three—oh no—Robin!" I had landed well on the one foot but Robin's balance was not set for it, and he was off balance, and the two of us started falling backward into the Atlantic as I held onto him. I had no choice but to push us back up with my broken left leg.

It must have been a guttural scream right into Robin's ear but I succeeded in keeping us from falling into the ocean but I also learned one thing: you will only put weight on a broken leg once in life. I nearly blacked out as the ends of the broken bones jammed and ground together inside the sack of skin, and I pivoted on my good leg and swung around—still hanging onto Robin's neck—and sat myself down amidst the still-splashing waves and wet rocks.

Robin was very alarmed and for good reason and asked me if I was all right and I seemed to be getting my wind back, and said, "Go get help. Go get the fire department. I sat next to the chief at dinner last night. Go get him. You can't help me get up that cliff. They're going to have to carry me in one of those baskets. I can't put weight on this leg again, that's for sure. You go get help. Let me see if I can move—yes—I can drag myself backwards and drag the broken leg and pull myself up out of the water. Go get help. Go now."

"That I will, old pal. You're sure you'll be all right alone?"

"I'm sure. I'm fine. My head is clear. I can think. My body is just going into shock, I can feel it, but it's okay, it's easier to take the pain in shock because the body shuts down. The body is great."

"Okay, old pal, I'm on my way, Jesus, we'll be back. I'll send Roger with a blanket. Your hands are cold."

Robin went for help and I crabbed myself backwards, dragging my broken leg over the rocks and the technique worked. Dragging a broken leg pulls it straight and takes some of the pressure off the broken ends inside the leg although any movement whatsoever is excruciatingly painful (the body is telling you: don't move that leg!).

I got myself out of the salt spray and up past the wet rocks and sat in a dry spot near a little bush. I felt the shock continue to engulf me and my breathing became shallow and my hands and body were wet with perspiration. I figured my blood pressure was about a hundred over sixty and my pulse was about fifty. Everything around me seemed sparkling clear in the bright moonlight and the silvery water below me bellowed out loudly with every crashing wave. I felt a great calm come over me as I adjusted somewhat to the intense pain, and for some strange reason I imagined I was a Civil War soldier that had been shot dead-center in the shinbone with a musket ball which shattered the bone. I imagined the enemy coming over the water and along the shore after me, and I decided I could still pull myself further backwards under the bush and sit there, and hide, and wait, and still shoot back if confronted. Yes, I thought, I could still fight no matter what the odds or circumstances, and the calm which I felt reassured me as I sat there—still—a silhouette against the brush in the bright moonlight—glancing occasionally at the ever-swelling leg which lay before me and which, thank God, wasn't bleeding.

"Jay! Jay!" It was Roger, Robin's son-in-law.

"Over here," I said, and as I said it I realized my voice was weaker than I thought. Yes, the calm had set in and I suddenly felt very weak, yet my mind seemed, still, very clear and sharp.

"You're cold. Here, let me cover you with this blanket. I've brought you a wool blanket."

"Careful," I said.

"Feeling okay?"

"Good as can be expected."

"Fire department is on the way. They're going to drive a truck to the edge of the cliff, and they'll carry you up in a basket. As you know, there are no medical services here, and the nearest clinic is on Martha's Vineyard. But we've radioed the Coast Guard and they're sending a ship to pick you up, and they've decided it would be better to get you to the hospital in New Bedford."

Yes, I thought still thinking of the Civil War, I could still fight for my country, yes, it's great to be an American. "The Coast Guard is going to help me?"

"It's all set. They're on their way. We don't have a boat here that's big enough to take these waves and in your condition"—he paused for a second—"this is best. I'll sit here with you and keep you company until they get here."

The firemen showed up and splinted my leg with duct tape and a two-by-four. They carried me up the cliff in a basket in the moonlight, and it flipped upside down twice. It scared me. The second time it happened, I grabbed one of them by the shirt collar with my fist and said, "I go, you go." They regained their footing and we all laughed at the comic difficulty of the task as we continued, slowly but surely, to the top. Then I rode on the back of a two-ton, flatbed truck across the rocky field to the road, and as my leg bounced around I thought of Lieutenant Henry and the ambulance in Italy in *A Farewell to Arms*. Well, it was better than a Civil War horse, or a wagon with wooden wheels, I thought, as we got onto the road.

At the dock, the Coast Guard was waiting, and it was one of those super-fast drug-dealer-chasing cruisers with some huge cannon or machine gun on the front which was covered in canvas. The ten-man crew was fully armed with ten-millimeter, semi-automatic pistols. With saluting punctuality and form, the crew took over, and I thanked the firemen, and they left. Robin Moore was there and said to me, "You've never been so well guarded in your life."

I felt honored as they put me into one of their baskets and carried me onboard, heading down into the lower cabin.

I wanted fresh air and didn't want to ride in the cabin, so I asked, "Can I ride back here on the deck with you guys? I want to listen to the engines."

Yes, of course, one of the men replied, and in another moment, we were on our way, the engines roaring at about three-quarter speed, which must have been between forty-five and fifty-five knots. We were moving very fast, and the ship took the waves at that speed as if there were no waves at all; it rode like a Cadillac on the silver water.

"What size are these engines?"

"Twin 908 cubic inch V-8 diesels."

"Wow," I said. They sounded great.

I was happy when we got to the dock at New Bedford, and thanked the Coast Guard wholeheartedly. I was happier still when I rolled into the emergency room at the hospital: medical attention at last.

There was quite an assembly of the night emergency room crew who had been expecting me for hours. You can imagine the radio traffic about my rescue up the cliff and the Coast Guard and everything, and I guess it threw the supervising nurse when I smiled as I caught her glance.

"You mean you're the guy with the broken leg?" she said contentiously.

Gawd, I thought, I guess she expected me to be delirious or something, or cringing in agonizing pain (it hurt like hell, I just didn't show it). She just couldn't understand how I could be happy. Maybe she thought I was on LSD or drugs. I just held my hands up as if to look at them and make sure I was really me, and then I said to her, "Yes. It's me."

"Well," she huffed in exasperation, "Are you *sure* it's broken?"

I rolled my eyes. Some people just don't get it. It seemed to be in the air of the summer. "Ma'am," I said, "I was born with one knee in my left leg. Now I have two. And the new one is between my regular knee and my ankle."

She snorted and called out to the others, "Give him a shot of demurol and get his vitals."

Before she could storm off I said, "Ma'am, just a minute. I don't need any drugs. I'm fine with the pain. I don't want any drugs. What I need is an x-ray and an orthopedic surgeon to come here and set my leg and put a cast on it. It's not compound and shouldn't require surgery."

"Heavens! Take him to the x-ray room!"

The x-rays didn't take long and the technician—who'd heard the entry conversation with the supervising nurse—exclaimed, "We're not supposed to render opinions, but"—he laughed and shook his head—"your leg is broken big time!"

"I know. I know. That nurse was nuts. You think I'd waste the time of all you people who've helped me? The Coast Guard even helped me."

In contrast to the nurse, the surgeon was great. "Simple fracture," he said. "All we need to do is set it and cast it. I notice you've refused pain medication."

"Yes. I wanted to be clear-headed."

'Well, you will be. You want me to set this without giving you medication?" he asked incredulously.

"I don't know. Can we do it?"

"That's up to you. I think you can if you set your mind to it."

"Let's try it."

And he started straightaway. "Sit up. We're going to move your leg to the side of the bed and let it hang over the side, which will help pull it straight. Next, I'm going to pull on your ankle with one hand, and feel the bones at the break with the other, and push them around there, too, a little, if I have to. Let's go, get your leg around, that's it, yes, I know it hurts to move, but pretty soon here we'll have it set and get a cast on it and—"

All I could think of was another Hemingway story and a war which I'd never been to, and when it was over I was proud and happy and soon there was a beautiful white cast, and then there was Robin Moore in the room with me, who'd come to help me, and I thanked the doctor and asked for Percoset so I could finally escape the pain for a while. Robin took me to his daughter's house where I could stay the night and get some sleep. It was after three AM.

It took five full days for me to recover enough to travel back to Wyoming on a plane. My brother and sister-in-law, who lived in nearby Connecticut, picked me up in their minivan and helped me recover enough for the flight. When I finally went, it was difficult and painful. People at the airports and in the plane bumped into my leg cast and my wheelchair regularly. I think they thought that a leg cast is like armor, but it's not. Just tapping the cast with a pencil hurt enough to get my attention. So when they walked into me, it really hurt. I would say, "Can't you see this huge, white cast?" But they didn't know that they had caused pain, so they ignored my comments, and I just had to put up with it.

The next seven weeks I spent in bed. Pissing in a bedpan, and basically bedfast, I sat still for the first time in my life.

"Now maybe you'll slow down and think about what you want to do with your career and this publishing company," Robin said to me over the phone.

And think about it, I did. I had tough decisions ahead, compounded by the fact that I was crippled for months. Some of the authors I had published over the years rallied behind me and helped me any way they could, Robin included. There were royalties and rights issues and they made deals with me to help the company stay in business. I had some corporate debt, and I was forced to sell a majority of inventory on remainders (taking huge personal losses to do so) to pay the debts, and even AAP worked with me regarding membership and dues. These people and the things they did to help meant a great deal me.

But, of course, there were those who were shrewd and took advantage to make money off the misfortune. Those people know who they are, and it was even one of the remainder buyers who promised payment and then reneged, and forced me to seek legal injunction to get the long past due money—which, after all—was promised to others.

There was also the continual issue of how my leg was healing. My regular physician, who recast the leg every week or two, said it was healing slowly, but doing fine. Another orthopedic surgeon, however, said it needed surgery, and that I would never be able to run again if I let it run its course without it. In my forties, I had been a runner all my life and could still run the mile under six minutes the day I broke it. So this was quite a contrast. I stuck with my regular doctor and rode out the casts. The surgeon, however, pounded me with huge bills just for seeing him and it was absurd. It was the same amazing contrast: those who saw gain and those who helped.

Within three months my left leg shrank to the size of my left arm, with my knee totally locked up and my ankle totally locked up. After another two months in casts, there wasn't much left of it. When the last cast came off, I couldn't even stand without crutches. It was a very difficult time, indeed. I had to go to Phoenix for part of the winter to get out of the snow and ice, and avoid the risk of slipping and falling with the crutches

I spent several months in Phoenix, and while I was gone I missed a very important call. Stephen King had called and wanted to talk with me. But he didn't leave his number and by the time I got the message he had quit calling. I decided to let it go until my leg healed, and when I got back to Wyoming I found his number in Maine and called. But whatever he wanted or had for me, it was too late (and then, about a year later, he was hit by a van and he had a broken leg). Suddenly, he must have learned what I had felt like. Life was full of irony and just strange all around.

And then, there was another twist which I had yet to look into. While I had been in Phoenix, Fate opened another strange door. I received an order from the Phoenix Library for *Lost Dutchman Mine Discoveries*, a book I had written and started the company on in 1988. It was odd to get the order because Phoenix Library usually ordered the book from Baker & Taylor. Since I was in Phoenix, I decided to pay a personal visit to the library to thank them for all their business through the years and to take some books to them personally. At the time I had just gotten out of the last cast and was trying desperately to learn how to walk again.

Somewhat comically, I managed to carry a few books and amble up a set of stairs and through the various sections of the library to meet the acquisitions staff.

When we met we discussed the plight of the local miners, who often stole the Dutchman mine book to get the full-color maps of the old Spanish tablets which I had photographed from a secret vault at the Mesa Southwest Museum. The library had to keep buying the book because of the continual thefts, and I asked why they had come to me directly instead of buying it from Baker & Taylor.

"Didn't you get the letter?"

"What letter?"

"Baker & Taylor is under a federal investigation right now."

"Really?"

"Yes. They've been short discounting libraries. They've been overcharging us for years, and we audited them ourselves and discovered that we were cheated out of seventeen thousand dollars last year alone."

"Can I see this letter?"

She got the letter and I read it, and then I explained how my company had been short discounted also, and that it all fit. In my opinion, they were cheating at both ends, cheating the publishers by taking huge discounts and then cheating the libraries by not passing along the proper discounts to them. The letter was signed by James Ulsamer, President of Baker & Taylor, and informed the libraries of the "audit" (investigation) by the government and that the libraries should cooperate.

"Well, well," I said as we concluded our meeting. "I'll just have to find out who's conducting this audit within the government, because this practice of theirs has really hurt me. And it's fraud, in my opinion. I gave them a 55 percent discount so that you librarians can get your full trade discount of at least 40 percent on my books. So we've both lost, and I intend to find out about this audit."

So I went back to Wyoming, and there I was, crippled, limping terribly, and sad about the missed calls from Stephen King. It was rough and I had no idea how hard it was going to be to bring back a leg which had been broken and in casts for five months.

One of the first things I did was call my senator's office, Senator Craig Thomas, R-Wyoming, and asked that the congressman make formal inquiries at the Justice Department and Federal Trade Commission. I was given assurances that inquiries would be made, but the congressman preferred that the inquiries be "informal." I agreed to that to see what would happen, but I thought it strange that they would not be formal.

Nothing happened. Neither agency disclosed anything, and the Federal Trade Commission even went further into secrecy, noting that they were under no obligation whatsoever to disclose anything at all to the senator. Dead end.

I worked and worked to try to get my leg back into shape in Wyoming. I was extremely humiliated, to go to the track and only be able to hop a dozen yards and then stop, because of the pain and weakness. But I hung in and kept at it and kept working the leg and trying to stretch out the joints. It still looked ugly at the break, red and swollen wherever the sock line was, even the pressure from the elastic on the sock caused inordinate swelling.

I knew what I had to do. I had to go to New York and find out what I could about the "audit" of Baker & Taylor.

So I went to New York City. Hobbling around in the airports, and at least able to get into a cab, I checked into The Metropolitan Club.

The next day I met with Jim Milliot, newswriter with *Publisher's Weekly*. I explained the situation with Ingram and the questions of fair trade and monopolistic practices.

"We've been wondering about that here at PW for some time now. Their dominance in the industry is without question, however the question is, *when* will something be done about it? And it may take some litigation to affect any change." Jim went on to discuss the matter further with me and added that he might do a story on it.

Then I brought up the letter from Baker & Taylor, which I'd seen at the Phoenix Library and the short discount issue. Jim was shocked at the treatment and said he'd heard rumors about the government audit, but didn't have anything confirmed about it. I explained that at least one of my books had been short discounted to the libraries, and to the trade bookstores.

"Which book was it?" Jim Milliot asked.

I handed him a copy of *The Moscow Connection* from my briefcase, and at the same time said, "Thanks again to you and your kind staff for your review. And thanks also to those at *The Library Journal*. It was the lead, feature book review in the November issue. Too bad we didn't get the sales we deserved, and that the libraries got gouged on the copies they did buy."

Jim held the book and looked at it curiously—reading some of the book review quotes on the dust jacket—and then looked at me inquisitively. "Do you think the content of the book had anything to do with the short discounting?"

"You know, I don't want to get into conspiracy theories or anything, or get labeled like that, but I must tell you that at the time, I certainly felt so. I really believe it was an act of censorship to stop the book in America. And I'm not the only one who's been the brunt of such activity in the news. Ask Gary Scurka, a former producer for Connie Chung."

Once again, Jim pondered the situation, still holding the book and eyeing it curiously, and suddenly, and softly, he asked me, "Do you know who owns Baker & Taylor?"

"No," I said, thinking, and then recalling something I'd heard, said, "Well, yes, I think it's the W.R. Grace Company, here in New York."

"No. No no no no no"—he paused and looked at his watch—"it's still open. Just a moment. I want to get something from our library."

He disappeared and came back a few moments later and produced several photocopied articles from the news including *The Wall Street Journal.* about Baker & Taylor. He handed the file to me and I read through it, first with looks of amazement, then of reflection, and finally a look of shock.

"Who's buying Baker & Taylor?" was the headline in the *Publishers Weekly* article, and the byline read, "With close ties to government, the four-year-old Carlyle Group has made acquisitions worth $1.2 billion and intends to make its newest the world's largest single source of English-language books." PW "decided to learn a little bit more about the Carlyle Group," and reported them to be "a private merchant bank and investment firm in Washington, D.C., that has major ties to the White House and national politics. Co-owned by the company's board of managing directors and the Richard King Mellon 'family interests,' the Carlyle Group was founded in 1987 and is headed by Frank Carlucci, whose background includes decades of top-level government service, including his most recent positions under President Reagan as Secretary of Defense (1987-1989) and as Assistant for National Security Affairs. (He was also Deputy Director of the CIA from 1978-1981.)." When I read this last I instantly thought of Larry Lunt and his book on Cuba which I published, and his release from Cuba in that same time frame. I was sure Carlucci knew who I was and about my books.

The article went on: ". . . David Rubenstein, a managing director, who—during the Carter Administration—served as Secretary of the Treasury and Chairman of the Federal Reserve Board. Also associated with the investment firm, in a senior advisor capacity, is Frederic V. Malek, who was appointed by President Bush to direct the 1990 Economic Summit of Industrialized Nations; he also served as director of the 1988 Republican Convention and in various 'policy-level positions' in the federal government." In addition, it was confirmed that Gerald Garbacz was "the person responsible for bringing the book wholesaler to the attention of the Carlyle Group. (Garbacz, who ran Baker & Taylor before moving to Grace, is also said to have White House connections, in the area of defense, dating back to the Kennedy Administration.)" D'Aniello was quoted as saying, "We'd like to expand on what we think is one of the more formidable assets in the industry, making Baker & Taylor the single largest source of English-language books in the entire world." That was one article.

The next was from *The Wall Street Journal.* The article named Secretary of State James Baker as an up-and-coming partner in the Carlyle Group which it described as a politically connected merchant banker. The article also stated that Mr. Baker's longtime protégé, former White House Budget Director Richard Darman, had recently been named a managing director of Carlyle. It also named former Defense Secretary Frank Carlucci as its chairman.

Next was another WSJ article: This one named international money manager George Soros as investing $100 million in Carlyle. They quoted Mr. Rubenstein as calling it more of a partnership than an investment.

Yet another article, the most recent, was dated the Fourth of July, 1994, and ran under the headline "Garbacz Departs as B&T Revamps Top Management." Reportedly, Carlyle had tried to sell the company to Follet Corporation, and the deal fell through. Garbacz had resigned, and Carlyle named three people to succeed him. Wow, I thought, this was exactly the time-frame of the launch of *The Moscow Connection.* The "new management" would have been the people involved in the events that summer and fall resulting in the short discounting of the book and the corresponding effect of censorship. Maybe it was one of their names that Jean Swope refused to give me as the person who directly manipulated our title information creating the fraud.

"Jee—mi—nee," I said, and let out a long sigh as I sat back in my chair.

Jim Milliot smiled wanly at me and said, "Interesting. Isn't it?"

I was stunned and just sat there for a few moments in silence, staring, of course, at my feet, and then I leaned forward in my chair and looked up at him. "The implications of this are horrifying. I've been cheated, and censored, and libraries have been cheated, and in a way censored also, by a company owned and operated by some of the most powerful political people in America. James Baker, former Secretary of State under Ronald Reagan? Frank Carlucci, former Secretary of Defense under Reagan and Deputy Director of the CIA under Director George Bush in the Carter Administration in 1979 when the author of my book on Cuba got out of prison? I'm sure they all know who I am. I'm sure Carlucci knows who Larry Lunt is. He'd have to. Lunt was CIA in prison in 1979. Then there's David Rubenstein, former Secretary of the Treasury and former Chairman of the Federal Reserve Board. You would think he would know percentages well. And millions from George Soros. If I think about it, every one of these people have a direct interest in the content of *The Moscow Connection*. The book details the counterfeiting by Russians which forced us to change the hundred-dollar bill. Nuclear weapons sales to terrorist nations. Russian crime moving into Jewish districts in New York City. My, my, my."

Jim smiled again. "Well—there you have it."

"Yes, I do. Thanks Jim. Gawd. Carlyle Partners—in Washington D.C.—what are they doing buying one of the largest book wholesalers in America, possibly to become the largest distributor of English language books in the world?"

CHAPTER TWELVE
One Flew Into the Cuckoo's Nest

Washington D.C. was hot and humid as usual that summer of 1996 when I arrived at National Airport in the afternoon. My friend and international attorney, John, picked me up at the airport. His response to it all was simply a low and barely audible sound: "Wow."

John described the size of the Baker law firm in D.C., and of course, the size of it in Texas. I spent the rest of that day and that evening with John, socially, and the next morning, I set out to wear off the heels of yet another set of shoes on the concrete sidewalks of the nation's capitol. Of course, my leg hurt so badly that I limped, which I tried to hide, and riding in cabs and on airplanes exacerbated the injury even worse than walking on it. But walk and ride I did. God, would it ever heal? Would I ever run another 10K, or the mile under six minutes? I couldn't know yet, or even really think about it. Whenever the pain affected me I tried all the more to stay focused on the business at hand: expose the censorship and save the publishing company.

First, I had to go to the equivalent of the Secretary of State for the District of Columbia to get the public information available on the Carlyle Group, and it matched *The Wall Street Journal.* information perfectly. I closely scrutinized the details of the articles and public records—as closely as scrutinize anything I read—like the way I notice that the period after the words *Wall Street Journal.* is part of their name, which most people don't, and I always try to include the period when I refer to that newspaper. Some would see this as a typographical error rather than extreme attention to detail.

Next, I went to the Federal Trade Commission, requesting a meeting with the Director, and while waiting to confirm, researched their files and disclosure duties and requirements. I discovered that there was no duty for them to disclose to the public any current or ongoing investigation, even with Freedom of Information Act requests. Further, there was no oversight committee. The Commission was very free and autonomous in the federal government. However, I found a rule which specifically required the FTC to give full disclosure to the Chairman of any Senate Committee or Sub-Committee. I photocopied the rule, 16 CFR Ch. 1 (1-1-96 Edition), number 4.11 (b) *"Requests from congressional committees and sub-committees.* Requests from congressional committees and sub-committees for nonpublic material shall be referred to the General Counsel for presentation to the Commission, subject to the provisions in 5 USC. 552(c) and FTC Act 21(b) that neither the Freedom of Information Act, 5 USC. 552, nor the Federal Trade Commission Act, 15 USC. 41, *et seq.,* is authority to withhold information from Congress. Upon receipt of a request from a congressional committee or sub-committee ..." I highlighted these words from the law in bright yellow.

I then called my Senator, Craig Thomas, R-Wyoming, and Senator Thomas agreed to see me the next morning. Senator Thomas already knew the business at hand regarding the short discounting, and had already made informal inquiries at various agencies. I was confident that since Senator Thomas was Chairman of a sub-committee in the Senate that he would make the inquiry to the FTC upon my request.

When I entered the Senator's office, however, there was a brevity in the air that seemed tense. Rightly so. The Chief Counsel for the

Senator attended the meeting and I read the rule. Highlighted in yellow, Mr. Thomas asked me to hand it to his Chief Counsel with words to the effect of, "Look into this and see if it is accurate."

I was quick to point out that it was not only accurate, that it was the law, in plain English, and that the Senator had the full power to make the request, and that the FTC had the full legal duty to disclose. I could tell by the meeting that the Senator was reluctant to make any formal request under the rule, even though I had proven his authority to do so.

Sure enough, the Senator refused to make the inquiry, getting word to me that it was because the business of the inquiry was not the same subject matter as the sub-committee of which he was Chairman. I argued that the rule didn't say that it had to be, but it was no use. The Senator referred to what he called, "protocol," saying it was "not protocol" for him to do it. To me it was just another Republican covering it all up for a bunch of other Republicans, just as the Director of the FTC had done by standing me up for the meeting which was scheduled with him. None of them were going to give me any information whatsoever. So that was dead, and meant that once again, I had chased my own tail and wasted my time, even though I had found the smoking gun for my Senator to get the information I needed about Baker & Taylor and the "so called" investigation by the government.

It all looked swept under the rug—for—and by—the big guys, and me, the little guy, could not find one snippet of information about the government investigation of Baker & Taylor. That's power.

I went back to Wyoming and sulked, but I kept sifting through options. They all came up dry, until one day the phone rang and it was a tip. One of my contacts in New York (this one I must protect the identity of) came through—the Justice Department was about to release a statement regarding the investigation of B&T!

I booked a flight and got to New York as fast as I could. I checked into The Met Club, and the very next morning *The New York Times* had the story. But they played it way down and their reporters didn't even want to talk about it. But *The Wall Street Journal* had the story played up—the Justice Department had joined suit with a suit filed under the Whistleblower Act by a librarian against Baker & Taylor in which the suit claimed B&T had cheated American libraries out of millions of dollars.

The news release about the lawsuit was quoted in the 1996 *WSJ* article titled, "Whistleblowers charge book company cheated libraries, schools and others out of millions of dollars." In the article, the *WSJ* states that Baker & Taylor is accused in a lawsuit by two whistleblowers of cheating libraries, schools, and government agencies out of millions of dollars over a ten year period in a book-selling scheme. The article quoted the news release which stated, "The US Department of Justice has been investigating the matter and filed notice on Jan. 31 in federal court in San Francisco that they will join the case.

"For at least the past 10 years, the whistleblowers and the government charge, Baker & Taylor has been deliberately mis-categorizing certain books on their computerized invoices so that customers that buy books with public funds are not given the large discount rates for trade books that the company has promised in its contracts. Instead, those customers were receiving a very small or no discount on those books...."

"I knew it!" I said to myself. "They did it to me and now there's a suit by the government." The news release, and all subsequent news I ever saw on the subject, however, kept the ownership by the Carlyle Group, and all the names of some of the most powerful Republicans in America out of the articles. So James Baker and Frank Carlucci and David Rubenstein and George Soros remained in the quiet background as B&T finally took some mud in the news for the accusation of cheating one of America's most precious institutions:

the library. Of course, I knew about the publishing and bookstore side of the cheat, but I still couldn't get that out in the news.

And what about censorship? Who was looking at the short discounts, title by title, to see if subject matter was an issue?

And last, the icing on the cake was that the investigation was handled by—not the FBI or Justice Department—but by the Department of Defense! Who in the world pulled that one off. Get the DOD to investigate some of its own former people? Why? One possibility is that it could be kept quiet that way. I could vouch for that.

It wasn't long after this that I was able to reach a settlement between Affiliated Writers of America, Inc., my publishing company, and Baker & Taylor Inc., as a result of discussions with Jim Ulsamer, president of B&T. We agreed to announce that we had settled our differences "amicably" and would continue doing business together. And he kept his word and his part of the agreement. It was a very good turn of events for both of our companies, and I worked very hard to rebuild my publishing house and make up for the lost years of business and the lost contacts and the lost momentum. I think also that it was very good for every small publisher in America because it set an example that there needed to be more fair distribution for smaller houses. It meant a lot for free speech. It also resulted in Baker & Taylor rising in popularity and use by bookstores, which increased availability of small press titles to the chains. It did not, however, change the way the rest of the industry would continue to do business.

What did make a huge difference in free speech however, and in book distribution, was the Internet. We are in an information revolution, and have been for several years.

In 1994 I tried to sell *The Moscow Connection* to Amazon.com, a new company which hadn't yet made its huge mark on book distribution and sales. They would only buy from one very large wholesaler: Ingram Book Company. Amazon.com had bought the database for Baker & Taylor titles for exclusive use on the Internet, and were therefore advertising some 3.1 million titles on their website, yet only about 400,000 of them were actually available from Ingram.

When Barnes&Noble.com opened their website, they attempted to offer as many titles as they could, and then filed suit against Amazon.com for advertising titles they didn't actually offer for sale. Suddenly, I got a call from Barnes&Noble.com asking to buy from me two copies of each title which I had in print. Amazon.com suddenly called and wanted the same thing. So the Internet forced at least part of the monopoly of book distribution to bust open. Many years later, in 2006, Amazon.com sells not only all the titles available through Baker & Taylor but also those from many other wholesalers and distributors and even publishers. I feel that I have been influential in the ability of Baker & Taylor and the other wholesalers to get their books into chainstore availability.

This doesn't mean that books don't still get buried and censored. It still happens and it is very clever, even more clever than the stories in this book. So, for anyone looking for controversial books, you may have to dig through rocks on the Internet to get them. And who really knows what power exists within governments or powerful, corporate entities (such as Google) to block searches and websites without the owners or authors knowing they are blocked and censored. We see it everyday in China and Iran. How about here in the USA? It would be interesting to know, I mean, really know. The Internet was, after all, created by the Department of Defense.

Chapter Thirteen
The Russian-American: Act Three

The next year, in 1997, the front-page news was the story of the arrest of two smugglers from Lithuania for trying to sell nuclear weapons and missiles to undercover agents in Miami. I saw the news and read the story and called Gary Scurka.

"Read the news?"

"Yep."

"Doing anything about it?"

"Nope."

"That's what I thought. Did your source get out of prison last week?"

"Nope."

"Keep me posted. I'm writing the story about it all, you know. I'm just now in the scene, literally, when I first met you in New York. Remember that day?"

"Sure do."

"You're in it."

"Good."

I was channeling my time to write and kept up a steady progress. I had kept notes on conversations and events which served me well when it came to quoting people and conversations but in the back of my mind was this building of the news around the Lithuanian arrest, and I decided to watch and see how it all emerged in the news. I suspected that suddenly the news articles would begin to appear depicting Lithuania in some different light so that Americans would have the *right* image, not the one which glared out about nukes. Gary Scurka's source had said years earlier that this was going on in Vilnius but he was still sitting in jail and now there was this news.

It was only a week later when I got a phone call—after hours— and there was a message from Suzan Mazur. I didn't know her and had no idea who she was. She said she had been trying to buy a copy of *The Moscow Connection* in New York City and could not find one. She said she'd tried Barnes & Noble and Waldenbooks, and had been told it was unavailable. Would someone return her call and tell her where she could get a copy?

What a surprise! I burst out laughing when I heard this—what a surprise! It took me back emotionally to the day when the FBI agents couldn't get the book when it came out, and now it was years later and I'd settled with Baker & Taylor and nothing really changed. The book still wasn't available in New York City. I just, good God, just I—I don't know—had I had enough?

I called her the next day and got a recording, but then she called again and asked about getting a copy of the book.

"It's twenty dollars," I said, and I had decided after the short discounting and everything that had happened that I was going to get twenty dollars out of every last copy I had of that book. Robin—that book—was so rich—he was so brilliant—and I worked so hard to edit and publish—twenty bucks—that's it! That's what was on my mind. I'm still amazed at the richness of his writing. I continued, "If you need it overnight, then you'll have to pay the freight, but if you want it regular UPS, I'll pay the freight. If you give me a credit card over the phone, I'll ship it to you today."

"Twenty bucks?" she protested. "Barnes & Noble said it was reduced to $4.98 but that they didn't have any and couldn't get it."

I thought about this mysterious $4.98 book which they don't have and can't get. You can imagine how I felt as the publisher.

Gawd, how dead can you kill a book? Only $4.98, but you can't get it? Get it? It's worthless but nobody has any.

"It's available and in stock at trade price at one wholesaler, but Barnes & Noble won't order from them, I guess. What store told you it was $4.98?"

"Barnes & Noble at 22nd and 6th Avenue. But it's no longer in the store. There is not a single copy in New York and it can't be gotten here."

"I know that," I said.

"Well, Peter said I could get it from you."

"Peter? Peter Grinenko?"

"Oh, you know Peter? He says he's the main character in the book. And actually, I'm with *Newsday* in New York, and I'm working on a story, and Peter is in it and he said I should read the book. So could you send me a press copy at no charge?"

"I'll tell you this. I know Peter. And I'm the editor and publisher of that book. And that book was censored in America, and still is. And usually a publisher gives the press free copies because we hope you'll do a story on it, and we hope we'll sell some books out of it. But in this case, you can't get the book and neither can your readers. So what good does it do me? You want to do a real story, do the story of how that book got blocked in America."

"Well, the book will be part of the story, I mean we're going to be on the John McGlaughlin Show, and I'm going to do a piece for *Newsday*. So I'd like to read the book. But I don't use credit cards, so if I have to I'll send you a money order to pay for it."

"All right, all right, I hate to make you do that. I'll talk with Peter and then decide."

"I'd rather not bother Peter with this. I mean—"

"No bother, believe me, no bother. What's the focus of your story?"

"The Baltics."

"Where in the Baltics?"

She started in about the story and I interrupted her, "*Where* in the Baltics?" I asked again.

"You want to see the story?"

"Can you fax it to me?"

"Sure."

I gave her my fax number and in five minutes I was reading it. Naturally, it was about Lithuania. As if I hadn't known. The title was "LETTER FROM VILNIUS—A New Baltics Invasion: NATO, FBI and Hollywood." It was only three days old and from the Currents & Books section.

I called Peter and left a message and waited for him to return my call.

"Hi, how are you?" I said.

"Fine. Nice to hear from you."

"Susan Mazur called."

At the mention of her name the phone went dead. It was typical when conversations were about Russian nukes, and to me it meant that either Peter knew her name was too hot for his phone and he had to get on some other line, or it meant that he was going to record what we talked about, or it meant a whole host of other possibilities, all of which potentially had something to do with intelligence and national security entities. Who could know for sure? Not me. I just knew it was hot, whatever she was up to.

Peter called right back and we continued.

"Where were we?" he asked.

"Susan Mazur called and wants a copy of *The Moscow Connection*. She told me you were the main character and that you told her she should read it."

"Yeh. She wants to do a story on me."

"I told you this book would make you famous. She wants a free copy."

"That doesn't surprise me."

"I read her article about Vilnius."

"So did I. She's into all this hype about crime, and I told her someone's been playing with her peepee."

I laughed. "She wants a free book because she can't buy it anywhere in Manhattan. I explained that publishers give free books to the media in hopes that they do a story and that their audience goes and buys books. In this case, what good would it do? If she dug through rocks trying to buy the book in New York and couldn't get it, what good does it do me for a thousand people in New York to read her story when they can't buy the book? I can't make any money."

"Make her pay for it."

"Why don't you buy it for her. Give me your master card number."

"No way."

"You know, we got censored on this book in America, and I think you know something about who did it."

"Censored? How so?"

"Short discounted—trucks disappeared and went to the wrong locations—we couldn't get books into New York."

"I don't know anything about that."

"I haven't forgotten that you told me the book was good, and was accurate, and then you told CBS that Robin and I were full of shit."

"I never told anyone that you were full of shit. And if I thought that, I'd tell it to your face. Have I ever said that to your face?"

"No."

"There you go. And I never said it to anyone at CBS, either. What I probably did say was that the book was fiction. A novel. And that Yaponchik was as capable of selling nukes as I am of brain surgery."

I paused a moment, and then said, "The point of the book in fiction was not to point the finger at Yaponchik, Robin simply fashioned a character around his image in the news. As the editor, I didn't use his real name. We did use the catchy nickname of 'the Jap' though. And he didn't get arrested and convicted."

"That doesn't mean shit. Yaponchik was a moron, bragging about being bad, and when the news came out about him in New York portraying him as a 'thief–in–the–law' he should have stopped it right there and sued the newspapers. But he didn't. He was a criminal in Russia who went to prison for having a gun. And he came to the States and built a reputation around the big news. Why the big news? It was time for the FBI to put a Ruskie in jail. The FBI spent too much money gearing up for all this so-called Russian mafia crime in New York, and they had to have an arrest."

"The purpose of the book was not centered around Yaponchik, it was centered around the idea that the Russian nuclear weapons and plutonium are for sale to terrorist nations."

"Sale of nukes from Russia? None have occurred."

"Don't you remember the front-page news about the Russian couriers in Frankfurt?"

"I don't believe it. To date, not one has been sold."

I thought Peter was being ridiculous. "They were arrested with weapons grade plutonium deplaning a Lufthansa flight from Moscow at the Frankfurt airport! They had over a pound of it. And Viktor Sidorenko, the Russian Deputy Minister of Atomic Energy, was aboard the same flight! Come on, Peter."

"*The London Times* ran three stories saying it was a German and Russian conspiracy."

"Look. Today we are exactly where we were three years ago, almost to the day, when the couriers were arrested in Frankfurt. That was August 10th, 1994. Only now it's Lithuanians in Miami selling nukes. Margaret Thatcher attended a convention in Phoenix six weeks ago and said that quote, 'Nuclear weapons have been sold to Libya, Iran, Iraq, Korea, and Saudi Arabia.'"

"Well, they didn't come from Russia," Peter said. "It was probably the French who sold to the Thatcher Five. Did you hear Clinton's speech in Madrid?"

"No, about what, Lithuania?"

"Yes. And that the arrest in Miami by customs agents was all blown out of proportion by the news media, because it was the attempted sale of nukes which don't exist."

"Rhetoric," I responded. "I know a guy who's in prison for knowing about Russian nukes being sold through Lithuania by secret ops in the KGB."

"There's lots of guys like that. You going to believe them? He could say anything to get out of prison."

"That's not the point. Russian spies have been arrested in all those agencies within the past three years, and most notably Special Agent Pitts of the Counter-Intelligence Division of the FBI in New York was arrested last December as a Russian agent."

"All I can tell you is, lots of guys are saying stuff like this, and it's not true."

Enough of that I thought, and changed the subject. "Who are you working for now?"

"Two days a week, still, at the Brooklyn DA's office. Otherwise, just my businesses."

"What about the agency?"

"What about them?"

"Don't forget, I still have a copy of your 1099."

"Oh, that. I never *worked* for them. I gave lectures and seminars. I still do."

"For who else?"

"The State Department, the FBI, the CIA, universities. The last lecture I gave was in Chicago for all three at once: the State Department, The CIA, and Chicago University."

Then Peter brought the nukes up again, asking, "Have you spoken directly with anyone involved in the handling of nuclear material?"

"Yes."

"Good. Now, so have I, only in Russia. And almost as if there were a conspiracy, they all basically said the same thing. *Why would anyone get involved with a substance that is dangerous to handle, spend a lot of time finding a market other than government agencies hoping they would sell it to them, so the agency could say 'see, we told you it was happening' and not only that, they'll fail to tell you they offered you thirteen gazillion dollars for it.*"

I thought about a simple trapper I had met in Wyoming who had a simple life catching beaver and fox and coyote, and then a government undercover agent approached him and asked to buy eagle feathers. It was a slick entrapment, like an easy conversation where a sentence would come up like, *On your trapline, do you ever see any eagle feathers lying on the ground?* And here's the trapper, dirt poor and barely getting by, and now all he has to do is pick up an eagle feather and it's worth a lot of money, and here's the buyer, and the next thing you know he was arrested for killing some twenty-five eagles to sell the feathers to this undercover agent. Yes, the temptation was too great, and the government caused it. Yes, I thought, some Russian could be found, lots of them were in a similar plight of poverty, and they'd sell nukes for the right amount of money. Rather than tell Peter the story, I got right to the point.

"Why would they sell it? Because there are governments like Iraq who have real people who will pay big money to get it. And the temptation is just as real, and the material is there, and it can't be stopped."

Peter responded, "The people that are directly involved in the bomb-quality stuff, if it is ever discovered, you can go right back to the person who handled it. They refer exactly to the kitchen where it is refined."

"The professor that I interviewed from UCLA who did not want to be quoted in the news, went to Russia as part of Clinton's team of scientists to evaluate the inventory and security controls on weapons-grade plutonium. They reported back that there was little, if any control, and that it could be taken readily with zero accountability. Now what happened to that report? It was buried and Congress was denied access, and had to file charges to get it, and never did. Iraq would cut people's hands off and stuff them into parents' mouths to get it, extort, kill, kidnap, and of course, spend millions in a black market attempts to buy it, which is much easier than the previous means. It defies my sense of rational probability to think that it hasn't happened already, one way or another."

Peter still defended the Russians. "They wouldn't want to be part of it."

"Oh, now it's the *morality* of the Russian people that will keep this out of terrorist hands. In general, I agree only because I think people are moral all over the world. Specifically, though, that's not an issue. Because you can always find a bad apple in a basket if you look hard enough. And there are too many baskets."

"Yeh, like Mike Tyson."

"I saw it," I said, "What a goon."

"Okay. Then let's talk about the stupid."

"Forget Tyson," I said.

Peter went back to the nukes. "Somebody has to know how to handle it to steal it and sell it. It's not easy."

"Some people have eaten plutonium to show that it's harmless, even though it has been proven that just one molecule in the lung will absolutely cause cancer. So we're dealing with the whole population of Russia, 200 Million? And what's their opinion and knowledge of it?"

"People in Russia just came off this whole thing about Chernobel. Control is on top of control. Also, it's recordkeeping. Have I been in these places were it was designed, no, I have to rely on the Academy of Sciences who say they know about it. Why should these criminals deal with these products when it is morally wrong?"

"Because it's easy money, big money," I said.

"Not easy money. Not easy to transport. They could care less about all these secret police. You know what they care about? An apartment."

"That's what Clinton wants Americans to care about. And nothing else. Stay home—watch CNN—don't worry—we've got the world under control."

"They haven't got anything under control," Peter said.

"Except nuclear weapons?" I asked facetiously.

"Nothing, except they've made it difficult to get."

"But if the government people can set someone up and they're willing to sell, the real Iraqis can find someone to sell, and pay them, and get it bought."

The logic finally seemed to set in between Peter and I, and I asked Peter if he would collaborate on a book with me, including this book which I was writing as we spoke (which Peter already knew).

"How could we collaborate on a book? We disagree."

"The dialogue of our disagreement would be very revealing, I think. And we see who wins. We play fair, argue fairly, and see who wins. It would be a great story."

"Brooklyn is three million people. It is one of the largest cities in the USA. And they get a lot of federal funding. And if you're going to work for the Brooklyn DA's office, you're not gonna give your personal opinions."

"Then quit."

"I'm not ready to do that."

"Fine. Can you get us a meeting with the Director of the FBI?"

"Probably. Would I? Probably not."

"We could get to the truth of this. That's what's important. I suggest you call a meeting with the Director of the FBI, and you and I will lay the Gary Scurka story out on the table alongside that of Special Agent Pitts, and see what he says."

"Definitely not."

"Why not?"

"Not a good idea."

"I'd like to hear what he says. I think Gary Scurka's source is wrongfully in prison, and right about the KGB smuggling nukes through Lithuania and selling them to terrorist nations."

"How can you believe that? Trainloads of tanks have been shipped to the West and sold as scrap metal. Does that mean anything? No. Besides, the government is researching whether these Lithuanians, arrested in Miami, really had nukes to sell."

"So what if they don't? Others do. Do you believe that Clinton would tell the world if there were nukes or terrorists?"

"Yes. Absolutely."

I laughed. "I don't. Look at what happened to our book. Look. You could help me with a book—with this one—with another one."

"About what?"

"About crime in Russia, about business there and all these ventures—"

"Where criminality ends and government begins, who knows?"

"Okay. I get that. What about getting the details about that out to the public?"

"I've got forty invitations right now to speak. Talk shows, seminars—"

"That's what I mean. But you don't have a book. Every talk show guest has a book out. Haven't you noticed? *That's* how the guests make money. You don't have a book. If you had a book, if you helped me write this one, then you would have a book to sell, and you'd make money every time you speak or get into the news."

"Yeh, well, I don't know. Part of the problem is journalists."

"How's that?" I asked.

"Like Yaponshik. Journalists and law enforcement created this bad-assed image, and Yaponshik let it go to his head. You know what he did in this country? Nothing. But he listened to this and *became* worse."

"He was a criminal or he wouldn't have done extortion. Someone was beaten to death in Moscow. He's been arrested, tried, and convicted."

"That doesn't mean anything."

"Strange comment from someone who works for the Brooklyn DA's office."

"I told you already. The news. The journalists. Even the CIA. Look at Moynihan. Boost the CIA budget? For what? For thirty years we knew the shoe size of the premier's driver. But the one thing we did not know was that it was falling apart. We were being jerked around for forty years. And then Robin, who takes all the bullshit from the newspapers and puts it together in a book."

"Wait a minute. Wait a minute, no no no no no. That's not how you talked about it before we went to press. Because I asked you about it—and there wasn't one peep from you along these lines. Why now? The agency?"

"I gave a lecture for the agency. I don't work for them," Peter said.

"Lectures?"

"Yeh. FBI. Agency three times. State twice. Look. You know what a *legat* is?"

"No."

"Legal attaché at the Embassy for the Bureau. You know what G15 is?"

"Government pay scale."

"Yeh, well it's over a hundred thousand. Get it?"

"Get it," I said.

"Yeh, well, I can give you a name and he's full of shit. A little get together with federal agents. He jumped on the idea that the reason I was down-playing all this was because I was corrupt."

I nearly shouted, "You are downplaying all of this! But I don't believe you are corrupt. I just believe you're working for the government and it's your job. And now I get the drift that others are playing it up to create good jobs for themselves. You gotta do the book with me."

"Look. There's smokescreens everywhere. D'Amato. Latvia. Wonderful. A smokescreen. It was the Latvian Communists who turned their jackets inside out and became democrats. Worse than Russian Communists!"

"Look! Do the book!"

"Can't unless I quit. I'm not ready to quit."

"You've got a duty," I pleaded. "A lot of Americans are investing money over there—I know someone who's written over three-hundred joint ventures. Says even if Americans lose, it's better than the cost of another Cold War."

"They're gonna lose. Russians are great con artists. And, wherever there's a pie, *every* Ruskie who sees the pie will figure out how to get his finger in it, or, he'll muck it up until he does. There has to be something in it for everybody. That's what you don't understand. Every government official. Every employee down to the last truck driver. They all have to be in on the take. That's the way it is. You can't just go over there and do business without understanding it."

"Peter, we could go over sixteen marketing variables, one at a time, and five basics of management—*planning, organizing, directing, controlling, staffing*—and through a discussion of each—"

"I'll think about it."

Then, to my total outrage, an acquisition of Ingram Book Company by Barnes & Noble was announced. Public and industry outrage caused them to back out of the deal.

I was living in Aspen, Colorado at the time, and in the midst of my outrage I had met a nice young lady on a flight to Aspen. We had just happened to sit next to each other. We spoke casually, and after hearing a few sentences from her, I said something like, "You're Russian, aren't you."

The response was brittle: "Ukranian."

I was still interested in all of the former Soviet states, and always will be, and we continued to talk and it got more and more interesting. I mentioned that I had published *the Moscow Connection* and she mentioned that she worked with Leonid Kravchuk, the former President of Ukraine. "He is in Aspen now. I'm on my way to meet with him."

"And what is the nature of your business with him?"

"I help him handle his money in the US."

"He's the former president, right, the man in power when Yeltsin started the revolution."

"Yes."

"Wow. Then he was part of the change in power."

"Yes." There were three men who enabled the fall of the Soviet Union—the presidents of Russia, Ukraine, and Georgia. Yeltsin could not have succeeded without the cooperation of the other leaders, and Kravchuk was one of the three who changed the world.

We continued to talk and she explained that he was in the natural gas business now. I asked if it was possible that I could meet him and interview him.

"It's possible. I will give you the name of his American business partner and his phone number at the condominium where he is staying in Aspen."

As we deplaned, we shook hands and she had given me her business card with the brokerage firm in Denver, and on the back she had written the name and number for me to call.

When I followed up on this, there was some reluctance on the part of the former president to meet with me. I hadn't been told no, but there were several conversations toward making the arrangement.

I called my good friend, Dave Nicholas, in Laramie, Wyoming. He was the uncle of one of my corporate attorneys and also an attorney himself. Perhaps more significantly, Dave Nicholas was a statesmen of incredible magnitude, yet so humble in his ways that you would never know the extent of his statesmanship or the extent of his contributions to the world. Among other things, Nicholas had served as part of the attaché to the US Ambassador for NATO, living part of the time in Brussels, Belgium. We came to know each other when I published *Leave Me My Spirit* by Larry Lunt, and his nephew, Phillip, mentioned that his uncle was in Brussels, the same city where Lunt lived. Through this association, Nicholas was sent a copy of the book and it was arranged for he and Lunt to meet for dinner.

Later, when the former Soviet Union collapsed, Nicholas immediately made the decision to learn to speak Russian. He also participated in the creation of an educational exchange program between the University of Wyoming and Russian entities involved in teaching entrepreneurship and business for Russians interested in the transformation of communism into free enterprise. Nicholas traveled to Russia often, and primarily worked in Sarotov. He had been successful in helping create over 300 business ventures and his Russian constantly improved.

Nicholas and I had even traveled to New York City together once, staying at The Met Club, to meet with Robin Moore and discuss the possibility of another book on Russia. The book did not come to fruition, however, Dave Nicholas and I had kept in touch.

I called him and discussed the possible interview with Kravchuk. He knew a lot about the former president and Ukraine, and mentioned, among other things, the work between the US government and Kravchuk regarding the dismantling of nuclear weapons. He said, "I'll give you the name of the general who worked with him and the amount of money involved, if you get my drift. That will get his attention."

Yes. It certainly did. Kravchuk and I met one afternoon in his condominium with his fifteen-year-old grandson translating for us. The condo was lavish in the most tasteful way with marble floors and animal skins on the floor as rugs and hanging on the walls, and a large, curved staircase to the left of the front door, which I ascended with the hostess who greeted me at the large, tall, beautiful, formidable, front door.

Kravchuk sat solidly in a chair with the stature and demeanor commensurate with such a powerful and respected former president. He was solidly built and his voice was strong and stern with an unbending quality to it. His grandson was gracious and very smooth, brilliant in my opinion, a healthy-looking, handsome young man who spoke nearly perfect English.

The interview lasted two hours. It was fascinating. We discussed the nuclear weapons issues, and when the issue of Ukrainian submarines armed with nuclear missiles in the Black Sea came up—that—had been very sensitive. When the issue of Ukrainian transition to free enterprise came up, I will never forget Kravchuk's arms folded across his sturdy chest and his comment: "We must *force* the people to work!" I mentioned the motivational force driving free-market economies—profit—self-achievement—salaries.... It didn't strike a positive note with him. Perhaps he was right, I couldn't know, having never been to Ukraine. I had been invited to travel there as his guest and see for myself what I could see. But I didn't go. It's one of the things I still wish I would have done. Natural gas and the pipelines which carry it through Ukraine to Eastern European and European markets is the top political issue in Ukraine, and Russia and Ukraine often dispute the royalties to be paid from the pipelines. And I had just met Kravchuk, who was in the natural gas business.

But as irony would have it, Dave Nicholas went! He had accepted a position as an economic ambassador to Ukraine, and the next thing I knew he was living in Keiv. I will refer to him from now on as the Ambassador. We communicated occasionally by email, and I was very proud for him in his new position. I had mentioned to him that perhaps one day he would come across some interesting manuscript for me to consider for book publishing, and one day he did. He sent me an email describing the situation, and asked if he could forward my email to the author. I agreed.

It turned out to be a manuscript about a Ukrainian journalist by the name of Gongadze who had been murdered, and worse, skinned alive in the process. His wife and family had sought exile in the USA and although there was international outrage, not that much was publicized in the USA. The author of the new manuscript claimed to have proof that the murder was connected to a president there and allegations of the murder of journalists and corruption. The last part of this story is, the author would not send the MS and would only let me read it in person if we met in Berlin. I was not willing to fly to Berlin under such circumstances, and sensed tremendous danger with the entire proposition. I also wondered how well such a manuscript could do in the American market. For these and other reasons, I was reluctant, and then I heard that the author had suddenly disappeared.

Later, when a presidential candidate in Ukraine publicly declared he'd been poisoned by someone connected to Russia, Putin, or KGB, the price of free speech and writing the truth had gone up astronomically in Ukraine. When dozens of former Chechin officers who had taken up residence in many countries throughout the world were suddenly assassinated, and the question of Russian, Putin, or KGB involvement came up again. It seemed easy to me: the Russian bear was alive and well. And it seemed to me that Putin had tremendous world power.

This was exemplified when Russian tanks rolled into Georgia, our ally, right? President Bush did nothing, and although the tanks and invading troops stopped short of the capitol city, and eventually, when someone in Russia felt like it, retreated, the message had been sent to the world. There are two oil pipelines through that region which carry oil from the Caspian Sea to the Black Sea. There was a lot at stake, and there still is.

Ambassador Nicholas was discovered dead at his desk in his office one morning about a year and a half ago (2008). When I found out about it, I was shocked, and feel the subtitle of this book has significance. The Ambassador had paid the price, the ultimate price. My heart goes out to the family of such a great man. He had been accused by Putin of involvement and interference in the elections in Ukraine, and there were allegations that he'd been poisoned with a drug which is very hard to detect and which induces a heart attack. An autopsy had been conducted by the US government, but the results, to my knowledge, have not been released to even the ambassador's family.

Ambassador Nicholas had been best of friends for many years with Dick Cheney, yet even Cheney, according to the ambassador's nephew Phillip, is mum on the issue of poisoning and a possible connection to Putin and the results of the autopsy. And so it is that another circle in life completes itself, sadly so in this case. The world has lost a great statesman, I've lost a friend, and the family has lost a loved one.

CHAPTER FOURTEEN
The Russian-American: An Epilogue

In 1999, Peter Grinenko appeared before Senator Ben Knighthorse Campbell and the Commission on Security and Cooperation in Europe. Others who appeared gave statements also. The following are excerpts from the hearing, except that Grinenko's testimony is offered in its entirety. The content speaks for itself, especially about corruption and crime in Russia and Ukraine, and about the lack of media coverage. It is deadly for journalists to report news about corruption or politics in these areas, and if they do, it is usually a political weapon against someone which has been sanctioned by some powerful official or businessman. The cost of writing the truth is extremely high, and a lesson for America that we need to protect what we have left of our ability to do so without character, or literal, assassination.

Also, the Russian character relevant to crime and corruption is described in detail by Grinenko. Robin Moore wrote about Russian character in *The Moscow Connection* many years earlier, and I tried to get the book to the American public. You will see that we had it right.

BRIBERY AND
CORRUPTION IN
THE OSCE REGION

HEARING BEFORE THE COMMISSION ON SECURITY
AND COOPERATION IN EUROPE ONE HUNDRED
SIXTH CONGRESS FIRST SESSION
JULY 21, 1999

Printed for the use of the
Commission on Security and Cooperation in Europe

US GOVERNMENT PRINTING OFFICE
WASHINGTON: 2000

THE FOLLOWING ARE EXCERPTS FROM THE HEARING

OPENING STATEMENT OF
HON. BEN NIGHTHORSE CAMPBELL, CO-CHAIRMAN

Senator CAMPBELL. I am pleased to open this afternoon's hearing examining the issues of bribery and corruption in the OSCE region, an area stretching from Vancouver to Vladivostok. In economic terms, rampant corruption and organized crime in this vast region has cost United States businesses billions of dollars in lost contracts abroad, with direct implications for our economy here at home....

TESTIMONY OF PATRICK A. MULLOY, ASSISTANT
SECRETARY
OF COMMERCE AND COMMISSIONER

Senator CAMPBELL. When we try to pursue transparency in government, as an example, what are the difficulties we face in countries like Russia?

Sec. MULLOY. My understanding is that in Russia you haven't

had any traditions of transparency, and you have had a centralized authoritarian regime which acted arbitrarily and capriciously. They have been in power for 70 years, so it's really hard then to come in and free up a lot of the economy. The American economic system really depends upon a lot of institutional factors which keep it from becoming Darwinian in nature. Unfortunately, those institutions are not present in some of these countries. It is so important for us to help transmit some of those institutional reforms so that when we do push free markets and free enterprise, we also push some institutional restraints—such as restrictions on bribery.

Senator CAMPBELL. If they have never known any other way, they have nothing to compare it with.

Sec. MULLOY. That is going to be a real effort for us. That's why I think your idea of moving this up to a higher level is very important.

SENATOR CAMPBELL. You were mentioning when you talked about supply and demand, that on the supply side there are several countries that still give tax breaks for bribes?

Sec. MULLOY. Yes.

Senator CAMPBELL. Or not tax breaks, some kind of—

Sec. MULLOY.—tax deductibility—

SENATOR CAMPBELL.—tax deduction if you paid a bribe—

Sec. MULLOY.—paid a bribe as a business expense.

Senator CAMPBELL. What are the countries again? Australia you said? Did I hear you mention several countries?

Sec. MULLOY. Switzerland is one of them. That's an amazing one. You would think that country would know better.

Senator CAMPBELL. Luxembourg.

Sec. MULLOY. I have them Senator.

Senator CAMPBELL. That's all right. Just as long as we have those for the record. I would like to remember that.

Sec. MULLOY. Yes. Australia, New Zealand, Luxembourg, and Switzerland...

Senator CAMPBELL. Then let me ask you a two-part question. Are there governments in the OSCE region that have been particularly successful in fighting corruption, and have there been any major arrests or convictions of corrupt officials in those countries that you know of?

Sec. MULLOY. In the report that we just issued to Congress, we do not have any enforcement actions by other OSCE governments to report on.

Senator CAMPBELL. None?

TESTIMONY OF DR. LOUISE SHELLEY, DIRECTOR, TRANSNATIONAL CRIME AND CORRUPTION CENTER, AMERICAN UNIVERSITY

Dr. SHELLEY: Thank you for inviting my participation here. The Center for the Study of Transnational Crime and Corruption is an academic center at American University.

Senator CAMPBELL. Pull that microphone over just a little closer to you.

Dr. SHELLEY: But we also run programs in Russia and Ukraine to deal with the problems of organized crime and corruption. It started with private funding from the McArthur Foundation. We are now funded and administered through the Department of Justice. One of the foci of our research is on corruption throughout Russia and in Ukraine.

One of the most striking elements of the problem is the lack of political will to fight corruption. This is true not just in Russia and Ukraine; it is true of the other States in the NIS, and, to a lesser extent, in countries of Eastern Europe that are also a part of OSCE. As the Russian expression goes, "The fish rots from the head." That is what we are looking at. Many of the leaders of these Newly Independent countries have talent to address ethnic conflict. Some of them are more successful in promoting foreign investment, particularly in the oil sector, but they very much lack interest in dealing with the issue of corruption.

There are anti-corruption working groups that are operating at high levels in Ukraine and Georgia; but I would not say that this was an initiative that came from within those countries, but very much a response from external pressure from the United States or from the World Bank that these issues need to be addressed.

Increasingly, when you ask this question—"About how many people have been prosecuted from corruption?"—we are seeing some high level investigations of corruption, but it is often being used as a political weapon. That is how one politician gets at his enemy rather than really getting at the problem of corruption.

Senator CAMPBELL. Those doing the investigating are probably just as corrupt as those being investigated, in some cases, I suspect.

Dr. SHELLEY: Or those spearheading the investigations. This is a real problem in giving integrity to the issue of corruption. It is becoming increasingly a political weapon rather than an issue to be pursued for itself to eliminate corruption....

The privatization policies we have pursued may have made Communism irreversible, but they did not make authoritarianism irreversible. Lack of free elections. Because who has the money to fund elections? Independent media doesn't exist in many parts of the former Soviet Union because the oligarchs or other wealthy politicians have bought up the press; and a concentration of economic and political power are consequences of the corrupted privatization process....

We need to make corruption a central issue in the way we engage with countries of the former Soviet Union and Eastern Europe. It is not just a question for the business community and foreign investment, which is very important. But it is a question for our whole strategy of how we relate to these countries, because our failure to recognize earlier that corruption would be a major force created an impediment to the creation of democracy and free markets, has affected this transition process. In many ways, we have lost the window of opportunity that we had in the early 1990s....

All right. Complacency in government. In Russia, there has been a dramatic decline in the number of prosecutions of individuals engaged in corruption over the last decade, especially during this period of redistribution of property. People have literally been able to get away with almost everything.

TESTIMONY OF PETER GRINENKO, PARTNER, STAYSAFE SECURITY CORPORATION, NEW YORK

Mr. GRINENKO. Thank you.

Senator CAMPBELL. As with the others, Mr. Grinenko, your complete written testimony will be included in the record.

Mr. GRINENKO. Thank you. Mr. Chairman, I want to thank you for the opportunity to address the Helsinki Commission today on the issue of corruption in the countries of the Organization of Security and Cooperation in Europe. This is a subject with which I have been closely associated in three ways: through my experience as a detective in New York City, as a businessman in the OSCE region, and as an American with ethnic ties going back to Russia and the Ukraine.

Just a little about myself. My mother's grandfather was a gentleman in the Czar's army, and all the male members of her family were killed by the Bolsheviks. My mother was born in 1917 and married my father, a Ukrainian, in the 1930s. After World War II, they managed to escape to Germany, where I was born. I grew up in the United States in an extended family that spoke Russian, French, and English.

In my early years, I spent several years in the company of my great grandmother and her daughters. They told me about Russia—the value placed on culture and the morality that existed there before

Communism. Even then, I sensed that their values were different from my mother's. At the time, I didn't understand the reason for the difference. Then I went to Russia.

In 1987, after over 18 years in the New York City Police Department, I was thinking about retirement. Most of my career in the police department involved property crimes, with over 10 years in the Auto Crime Division. In 1980, because of my ability to speak Russian and the Soviet emigration in the mid-1970s, I had experience dealing with Soviet criminals in the United States. As a result, I was recruited by the FBI for a small task force that dealt exclusively with criminals from that part of the world.

Not only were we very successful in the investigations and prosecutions of these criminals, but this experience greatly enhanced my understanding of the Soviet mentality. At the same time, policies instituted by Gorbachev were opening up the Soviet Union. I already had a number of businesses in the United States. I thought that this was the perfect opportunity to use all my experience to get involved in a new and interesting venture in the land of my ancestors.

I visited the Soviet Union for the first time in 1987. By 1988, I had set up my first joint venture. I still travel there four to five times a year, usually a month at a time. I continue to conduct business in a small and limited way. The main reason that I have limited my exposure is the topic of today's hearing. Based upon my experiences, bribery and corruption in the former Soviet Union are not the exception, they are the norm.

While corruption existed before the dissolution of the Soviet Union, the collapse of political controls and the influx of hard currency have produced post-Soviet business practices that are even more corrupt. The purported advent of capitalism and democracy in that part of the world has not only made matters much worse, it has also had a much greater effect on the public in general.

In 1991, I shut down my largest enterprise, which included operations in Latvia, Russia, and the Ukraine, because I realized that there was no way for me to conduct business in these emerging economies without taking part in the corruption. Combine this with a substantial loss of product due to pilferage by factory workers, among other obstacles, and you begin to realize, as I did, that it was next to impossible for me to make a go of it.

However, I kept trying. Some call it wishful thinking on my part. More times than not, I ran into the same problems. For example, an enterprise in Russia requested I sell them equipment for a small meat-processing plant. I offered to set up a turnkey operation for $1.2 million. However, the Russian business people with whom I had negotiated on this project chose to accept an offer by an Italian company who set up a much smaller operation, but for $800,000 more than I had proposed. Why?

As I found out later, the Italian company had paid off the director and his assistants. Even though I didn't consider myself naive at the time, I was still flabbergasted by how blatantly open the corruption was.

It really bothers me to see what has become of the country that my great-grandmother used to speak of with such pride. It has become important to me personally to try to understand what had led to the current state of affairs. In over 12 years of exposure to the Soviet and post-Soviet system, I have learned that there were many contributing factors. Almost all of them can be tied to the effects of 70 years of communism.

The socialist ideal that everyone is equal did not stop people from wanting nice things; but it fostered an environment in which people could not get the nice things they wanted legally, so they resorted to illegal methods. People went to work not just for their salaries, but for what they could steal. They then used what they stole to barter for the luxuries, or sometimes just basic necessities that were in short supply.

By making the absolutely normal human desire to have a criminal activity, communism produced two generations of people for whom corruption became a way of life. Furthermore, there were the legal and sub-legal limitations on religious practices. To be a success in the communist system, you could not be known as a religious person. You could lie, cheat, steal—but as long as you could quote the latest party line and had the right friends, that was the ticket to success.

If you can imagine the result of the morality of that time, then today's situation is even easier to understand. The people who were responsible for all this are still in control now, but today they wear the jacket of democracy.

When I found out several months ago that I might be asked to speak before this Commission, I started questioning people about their personal experiences with corruption. This was not an easy task since most people don't appreciate it when you ask them things like, "When did you first become a thief?"

On one occasion I had a discussion with a woman in Russia. I told her about a case that I had worked on as a detective in New York. We had recovered a quarter million dollars. I explained to her how we went about handling the money. As we spoke, it became abundantly clear to me and to her that she and everyone that she knows would have handled the money very differently than we did. After our discussion, she realized how ingrained her corrupt attitude was and conceded that her attitude was probably indicative of the society in general.

When I asked another woman, a healthcare worker in Latvia, about her first experience with corruption, she tearfully related a story about her child (sic) on the kolhoz, which is a collective farm, in Belarus. She was about 8 years old, and her father used her as a lookout while he stole grain from the warehouse. She said her father excused what he did by saying that the grain belonged to the state and the people are the state. In addition, he claimed that it really wasn't stealing because the director of the kolhoz would also be taking some.

Corruption in this part of the world does not just occur in government. It is not just a problem when trying to conduct business. It is a part of the society and is perceived as a means of survival. Indeed, the situation even exists within the immigrant community in the United States. For example, immigrants from Russia who have organizational and managerial positions in the home healthcare field help more recent immigrants in obtaining the training and certification required for employment. They also help find positions for these immigrants once they are trained. At each step of the process, bribes are expected by the manager. If the immigrant does not have status—that is, an illegal immigrant—the situation is even worse. Typically, those without status are required to pay additional monthly bribes to the managers in order to keep their jobs.

My Chairman, I hope that my testimony has helped to personalize your knowledge of the problem that our business persons and law enforcement personnel face in dealing with corruption in the countries of the OSCE. I also know that the Commission and the Congress would like to hear proposals on combating this problem. I don't think there are any realistic short-term solutions to this problem. Hopefully, some of the legal approaches initiated by the international community to combat bribery will have some effect. But any long-term solutions must address society as a whole.

In my opinion, the only methods that have any real chance of working are those aimed at the younger generation in these countries. It is unfortunate, but it is my experience that most of the older generation have absolutely no confidence in their government or in their own future. They are just concerned with having as much as they can now; and in order to get it, they will do whatever they have to do.

Just teaching students from the former Soviet Union about democracy and capitalism won't work. However, it is my understanding that there are currently programs in which high school and college students come to the United States for a short period of time, go to American schools, and live in American families. I think this is a good idea.

Young people from these countries need to be exposed to our way of life—yes, even with its negative characteristics—so that they can learn about capitalism and democracy firsthand, so that they will get a historical perspective of our freedom and prosperity. They need to understand that delayed gratification and even sacrifice may be necessary before they make their first million.

They also need to see how basic morality and rule of law works to protect property and lawfully acquired wealth, that armed guards are the exception rather than the norm. Their experience here will allow them to see how destructive corruption and bribery are to the moral fiber of their society. Some of them may not be especially moved by these lessons, but I believe that many of them will return home and share what they've learned. With a large number of students and over a number of years, I am convinced that slowly, changes will occur.

When we send teachers to set up various training programs over there now, they are ineffective because the Russians laugh at our efforts. They look at us as naive and cynical Westerners, getting paid to come to address a culture that we know nothing about. I don't think they will be as quick to laugh at their own family members or fellow citizens.

These opportunities should be available to a large number of students on a continuing basis. I don't know how the system works, but insofar as the United States Government is a sponsor, I trust that there are necessary safeguards in place to assure that the selection of participants is equitable. Otherwise, only those children of the controlling elite might end up being included.

We currently send millions in aid, but those in power only use it for their own purposes. They have had 70 years of communistic teaching and have lived the reality of corruption. The next generation of Russians, Ukrainians, Latvians, et cetera, need to see another type of reality. I don't think they will see it or understand it unless they live it.

Mr. Chairman, our own security and economic interests are enhanced when crime and corruption are reduced in countries that we need to deal with. I hope this hearing will assist the Commission and the Congress in this endeavor. I will be glad to answer any questions that you or any of the members of the Commission might have.

Thank you.

Senator CAMPBELL. I thank you.

I have several questions. I am also going to ask all of you to respond to some of them in writing since we may run out of time. Before I do though, I would like to introduce Congressman Frank Wolf, who is a member of the Commission.

Thank you for coming over, Frank. Did you have an opening statement?

Mr. WOLF: No.

Senator CAMPBELL. I was reading your testimony while each of you were talking. Mr. Grinenko, how did you find out this Italian firm paid—they bid, or I guess they were charged—$800,000 more to set up a smaller operation. You discovered that there had been some payoff to the director and the assistants. How did you find that out?

Mr. GRINENKO. It's really simple. You would set out a bidding situation. You are dealing with the director of the factory or the plant. In this case it was—

Senator CAMPBELL. Did they tell you?

Mr. GRINENKO. He didn't. People from my side found out.

Senator CAMPBELL. But you had proof that that was done? It wasn't just rumors?

Mr. GRINENKO. Absolutely. I mean the amount of the money might have been exaggerated.

Senator CAMPBELL. You have been back a number of times to the Soviet Union and Russia. Let me ask you two things. Is the situation getting any better or worse in the number of times you going over there? What advice would you give to an American businessman if they were going over there to the former Soviet Union and trying to do business?

Mr. GRINENKO. I would suggest that the American businessman remain here and invest in the stock market.

But I wanted to mention one other thing. Dr. Shelley mentioned the independent media, and if they would encourage it. There have been several killings of reporters in Russia, unsolved, will never be solved.

Senator CAMPBELL. Is it your experience that the free media might be in jeopardy, but that there are other media that tow the line and are—some of the media themselves are involved in the payoff process?

Mr. GRINENKO. Yes, Mr. Chairman. It is that they have to support their families. I mean there are very few in the media that are going to risk dying, and many have died. There might be the intent to report, but it's not the reality.

Senator CAMPBELL. When the wolf is at the door, it's pretty hard to make all kinds of wonderful high level—

Mr. GRINENKO. Absolutely.

Senator CAMPBELL. Yes. When we were over there, the fellow that was driving our car was a physicist teaching at the local university. He had to drive a taxi at night to make ends meet. He told us that one of the custodians in his university was a thoracic surgeon. When things are that tough, I can understand how it's not too hard to look the other way if you thought you could get some money for it.

Mr. GRINENKO. That's right.

Senator CAMPBELL. You also mentioned that your investigative work in New York City enhanced your understanding of the Soviet mentality. How does that Soviet mentality play a role with respect to corruption? Is that how it was developed over 70 years of communism—that it is sort of ingrained? Is that what you meant by that?

Mr. GRINENKO. That is absolutely correct. It's just moved over. Under socialism, it was a little controlled, a little quieter, not as open. Right now it's wide open. I mean if there isn't some benefit derived for that person—whether it be a warehouseman, whether it be a cab driver—if there is something that has to be done, those people need to be compensated for it beyond getting paid.

Senator CAMPBELL. Fair enough. When we were over there, we visited the National Police Training Academy. I forgot the general's name that was in charge of it, but it's obviously conducted at least in cooperation with the army because the commanding officer wasn't a civilian policeman. He was a major general.

As I understood it, that police academy trains all the police from throughout all the Russian cities—the training goes through that central academy. It's not like the United States, where New York has an academy and L.A. has an academy, and everybody has their own. It's one centralized academy.

He told us that on one of his visits to the United States, while visiting the Chicago Police Department he noted there were three Russian criminals in jail in Chicago, which obviously led me to confirm what I had already believed—that the growth of Russian-American gangs and Russian-American crime is on the rise. Is that your belief too?

Mr. GRINENKO. That whole aura of Russian organized crime is a whole other subject. I mean, there are three people that really benefit or three groups that benefit from "Russian mafia." One, the journalists and the people that write about "Russian mafia."

Two, law enforcement, because they investigate very interesting, important criminals. The most important reason that there is a "Russian mafia" is because the "Russian mafia" wants to have a "Russian mafia", that is, the criminals involved. They use that. They use that aura to frighten others.

Are they organized? No. Are they structured? No. Are they criminals? Yes. Are they violent? Yes. But for the most part, the entire immigration—that is the Russian immigration—and what we're discussing has an overall economic effect on our society because of the amount of money that is scammed and schemed out of our system.

Senator CAMPBELL. Which way do you think the flow is going when you talk about—this is a little off the agenda, but I am interested in it—the flow of organized crime. Is the flow coming in this direction?

Mr. GRINENKO. Exaggerated.

Senator CAMPBELL. Does that come from Russia this way or do the American criminals recruit that way?

Mr. GRINENKO. The Russian criminals in Russia have a good time committing all their crimes and controlling Russia. For them to come over here—it's like for the longest time I had—people who were saying that they were recruiting Russian criminals to come here, kill somebody, and go back to Russia. It is like asking me to go to Taiwan to kill a Taiwanese resident. I wouldn't even know what bus to take or cab to call. The whole concept is ludicrous.

Yes, there are gangs. There are criminals. They are a part of the system in Russia. They are used. Prior to the coup, the criminals were used by government. After the coup, there was a little time where the criminals were getting more control. At the moment, we are back to the government and powers in the government controlling the criminals.

Senator CAMPBELL. There is a relationship between the government officials and organized or disorganized crime?

Mr. GRINENKO. Absolutely. They develop deficits. They can blame the criminals for it.

Senator CAMPBELL. Dr. Sullivan, let me ask you about the upcoming parliamentary elections later this year in Russia and the Ukraine. How do you think that that is going to affect the business climate?

Dr. SULLIVAN. The most fundamental problem with the business climate right now is the fact it's stabilized at about 24 rubles to the dollar. If they can keep it there, we'll see increasingly the small business, the medium-sized business, moving into a ruble-based economy.

They are actually not doing very badly. I put the same question to one of the vice presidents of the Russian Chamber recently, about how they saw their small business members faring. It wasn't bad. The big danger will be will it become destabilized. That is where the parliamentary elections and then increasingly the presidential election can throw a monkey wrench into the system.

As we saw in the last presidential election—in the wake of that election and the promises, the side payments, and everything else that went on with it did have that effect of destabilizing the economy.

Senator CAMPBELL. You were over there talking to a number of Russians that spoke English, that—I mean they were pretty open about some of the candidates that are running for president of Russia next year. One candidate in particular—he is just a known criminal. I mean, he has a record of corruption, a record of bribery, a record of being on the take, is a snake. Yet he is running for president. It seems like the people I talked to—the Russians I talked to—were fully aware of it. They knew it. Yet he has an inside chance—they say—of becoming the president of the country. My gosh, if that happens I think we are all going to be in trouble.

Dr. SULLIVAN. I am not sure exactly who you are talking about, but—

Senator CAMPBELL. I am not going to mention who I was talking about. I don't want to meddle in their internal business.

Dr. SULLIVAN. Three or four candidates come to mind, but I'm not sure that that is actually going to happen.

Senator CAMPBELL. One seems to rise to the level of heads and shoulders above the other ones, to the Russians I was talking to.

Dr. SULLIVAN. I am not sure it is going to unfold quite the way that anybody thinks. I mean the prediction horizon is really literally about 48 hours in Russia. Moving beyond that is extraordinarily difficult.

But this is something that traces its roots back to the Triple M scandal. If you recall some years ago, there was a pyramid scheme where a guy named Sergei Movrody ran a pyramid—just flat out stole money, no question about it—and then ran for parliament, got elected, and claimed immunity. So there is a tremendous incentive for people that engage in dubious commercial transactions to do that.

Senator CAMPBELL. Do you know the status of the former Ukrainian prime minister? His name was Lazarenko. I understand he is wanted by the Ukrainian government for corruption, by the Swiss government for money laundering. Do you know where he is? Has he applied for a visa or asylum or anything in this country?

Dr. SULLIVAN. Well, I know that he has applied. I don't know what the disposition of that was. That case kind of disappeared off the radar screen from my personal attention.

Senator CAMPBELL. He has applied?

Dr. SULLIVAN. He has applied. He was, I believe, arrested, trying to enter the United States. He was arrested in Switzerland using a Peruvian or Filipino passport, I remember, and then exported back to Ukraine, and then turned around and left and came here. But I don't know where he is now.

Senator CAMPBELL. Thank you.

Dr. Shelley, when we talk about some of the mistakes we have made, I know it's like un-ringing a bell, but do you think there are steps that the US business could have taken to deal with corruption in the emerging Soviet market? Do you think they are really aware of the pitfalls or did we just have this kind of pie-in-the-sky attitude that the new open markets kind of rush in pell mell without recognizing what we were going to have to go through as American businessmen?

Dr. SHELLEY: I think that very much we ignored this issue.

PART TWO

CHAPTER FIFTEEN
The Frog and the Scorpion

In the spring of 2006, as I was writing parts of this chapter in present tense, we were obviously at war in Iraq. The anniversary marking four years of war was yesterday. We were at war in Afghanistan. The Patriot Act had just been renewed by Congress.

And all of this mess and death could have been avoided, as well as our total loss of freedom in this country, as you will see in Part Two of this book. As I continued to write and update this section through 2010, it seemed that America was ready for some truth.

During the years from 2003 to 2006, if a person spoke out in public or in a bar criticizing Bush and Cheney for the way the war in Iraq was being conducted, they better be ready for a physical fight. It was literally dangerous to oppose policy on the war, and any such criticism or public commentary had been equated falsely by the White House as "not supporting the troops." This had to have affected the news media and what they were willing to generate in print and over the air. But it can also be considered that the media had fed this misconception between political criticism, patriotism, and supporting the troops. What if we went into Iraq under false pretenses? Guess what? We did. There were no weapons of mass destruction, and it became apparent that Bush and Cheney had intelligence on this, knew this, and went ahead with the invasion anyway. There were no links to al-Qaida and yet the invasion of Iraq was falsely touted as part of the War on Terror.

I saw all of this happening and wondered why the media largely ignored these issues and focused on presenting the party line. Now, in 2010, when I speak to someone about the war in Iraq in public, more often than not, they look around to see if anyone else is listening, lower their voice, and say, "I think it's disgusting." American opinion has changed, but policy has not.

The events which have kept me from writing and publishing this until now are also some of the events which bring it all together in the end. These wars are about oil companies and defense contractors making huge sales and profits—and allegations about profiteering and corruption abound. Overpayments to Halliburton, for example, proved out to be substantial.

In 2008 the book titled *The Three Trillion Dollar War: The True Cost of the Iraq Conflict* was published by W.W. Norton Company. The title speaks for itself: three trillion dollars by 2008. Joseph E. Stiglitz, one of the authors, is a winner of the Nobel Prize in economics. In that book, Halliburton is described as receiving sole-source contracts and cost-plus contracts which totaled at least $19.4 billion. How convenient that its former CEO, Dick Cheney, had become vice-president of the United States, the chief architect of the war in Iraq, and the chief architect of its rebuilding.

Also in the book, Halliburton's Republican Party contributions totaled $1,146,248, while the Democratic Party only received $55,650. After the war began, Halliburton's stock increased in value 229 percent. Lockheed Martin stock went up 105 percent. Isn't it interesting that Cheney had stock interests in both companies?

According to http://www.celebritynetworth.com/richest-politicians/dick-cheney-net-worth/ Dick Cheney's net worth is $90 million dollars. Other estimates place it between $30 million and $90 million, at an average of $60 million. It has to do with the way it is reported on tax forms required of executive-level officials. Donald Rumsfeld is the richest on the list, with an average net worth of

$137 million in 2004 (in 2004 Cheney came in at an average net worth of $47 million).

In a rare article on September 3rd, 2000, which ran in the Casper, Wyoming *Star Tribune* on the front page, Washington bureau reporter Jason Marsden wrote about Dick Cheney pushing for a $489 million loan guarantee in 1999 (when he was not involved in presidential politics) to a controversial Russian oil company. He tells the story of Tyumen Oil Co. (TNK) and how they sought a Western loan guarantee from the US Export-Import Bank (Ex-Im). The loan proceeds were going to be used primarily to buy equipment from Halliburton to develop an oil field in the Caspian region.

But the Russian and trade presses had reported TNK as a company who had just muscled into control of a Russian rival oil firm in the area, upsetting its top foreign shareholder and leader, BP Amoco. BP Amoco then commissioned a report linking TNK and its parent company (the Alfa Group) to the Russian mob and international drug traffickers. They also lobbied against the loan guarantee in the States.

TNK turned to Cheney, head of Halliburton and former Wyoming congressman and defense secretary "to work his Washington ways on behalf of the half-billion dollar taxpayer aid package," the English language *St. Petersburg Times* reported earlier that month. "He undertook a very strong lobbying campaign … Halliburton was very interested in getting the contract" to develop TNK's Somotlor field, TNK spokesman Andrei Krivorotov told the Russian paper.

Cheney's hurdles were high. At the time, Madeline Albright had put a hold on the deal "in the interest of national security"—just as US-Russian relations were foundering over the war in Chechnya.

But that was only part of it. According to the Center for Public Integrity (CPI), Halliburton, under Cheney's helm, had helped win its clients trade-bank guarantees totaling $1.5 billion in just five years.

The CPI's Internet magazine, "The Public I" (www.public-i.org), cited unidentified ex-Russian intelligence operatives and described the Alfa Group as "a KGB-founded front for looting state enterprises and channeling heroin and other hard drugs worldwide under the control of a Chechen mob family." The report also quoted anonymously an attorney at TNK's US law firm of Akin, Gump as calling the organized crime allegations "way off the mark." TNK's Washington PR firm of Fleischman Hillard also disputed the charges.

It is obvious to me that the first book in America with Chechin characters and Russian mob characters which carried a theme contrary to the agenda of Cheney and Halliburton could become a target for repression and censorship in America. One review described the book as a novel of near perfect motion, which depicts Russian criminal society and its mores, and also stated that Americans better get used to recognizing these men because they are going to be around for a while (*The Boston Herald*, Christmas Day 1994).

In any event, and of no surprise to me, after three months of consultations, the US State Department withdrew its objections to the loan guarantee. Cheney, or someone, had the power to pull this off in spite of objections. What happened to the information cited in this book from the Senator Campbell hearing? Apparently, it was largely ignored in the government, or at least in cases dealing with Cheney and Halliburton. Put that with the other loan guarantees, and Halliburton and Cheney made out quite well. In a broader sense, even, it fits that in the 1990s, secretaries of defense and former secretaries of defense involved in the military-industrial complex and the oil-industrial complex would not want a book like *The Moscow Connection* about the Russian mafia and Chechen characters to hit the American bookstands. Whoever was behind it, the book never got a chance in the market. Even when the *LA*

Times book review came out, I couldn't see where we got any sales at all in spite of all of my efforts to get the book into the stores and into trade distribution. The review itself carried a grave message: that the power vacuum created by the collapse of the Soviet Union was filled with a shadow government of vicious gangsters. When you look at the super-rich oligarchy in Russia today and look at how they amassed and took control of huge enterprises, especially oil, the prophesy rings true. And the oligarchy appears to be in a partnership with Putin and his government. It seems obvious to me that conducting oil business there amounts to doing business with the Russian mob. Cheney and Bush, in my opinion, had to have known this. Huge amounts of money through loans and guarantees were going to flow into Russian oil deals, and a large part of the money was going to flow back to Halliburton.

If we hadn't invaded with masses of troops and literally bombed the hell out of Iraq, would Bush and Cheney have been able to write the $19 billion check to Halliburton? And what about the other hundreds of billions in checks to the manufacturers of the bombs, airplanes, and helicopters—and major airlines who flew many of our personnel in and out of there, who were in financial trouble and had to be bailed out. And don't forget the oil companies that got their share directly for all the jet fuel and other fuels provided for us to destroy Iraq, and then rebuild it, not counting the astronomical profits on the doubling and nearly tripling of gas prices.

The cost of trillions of dollars to taxpayers, and substantial amounts of that money going to Bush and Cheney's pet Halliburton should be enough to make anyone sick. But the sickest thing about it all is how Bush and Cheney got away with it in the first place. My opinion is that these wars are about oil and an oil pipeline which needs to be built through Afghanistan and Pakistan to get Russian oil to the Arabian Sea and the American market. The seeds of the plans for this invasion are documented in 1995, when Exxon-Mobile made its pitch to a senate sub-committee hearing. But it didn't work out for Exxon-Mobile the way they had planned. When they made their big move to buy 25 percent of Yukos, the giant Russian oil firm, Putin stepped in, blocked the sale, and arrested the chairman of the board on "tax evasion" charges. It reminds me of how Al Capone got nailed. Putin then basically nationalized Yukos and Exxon-Mobile is out. Obviously, to me, Putin is too smart to let American oil companies reap the huge profits from their oil fields even if it was American money and Halliburton equipment that developed them. In my opinion, Putin outsmarted them all. They don't need our investment dollars now, they have plenty of their own capital and cash flow. And Putin has tightened the grip on free speech and freedom of the press in Russia, where it is very dangerous to be a journalist.

Correspondingly, there is no freedom of speech in America. Through the Patriot Act and the broadly interpreted powers of the office of the president by such attorneys as John Woo, the president can arrest and even torture people with little or no recourse available to the accused. Even though the past legal opinions of Woo to President Bush are now being described as intentional professional misconduct, it appears that little or no action will be taken toward Woo or to rectify the arrests and torture carried out in "black site" prisons such as the one in Thailand. Ultimately, Woo was judged by the Justice Department to have only committed "poor judgement," but no professional misconduct. Accountability in government is out the window. So *Newsweek* breaks a story on this in 2010. What happened to the story about this in 2002 or all the years that people were being censored for political views and tortured with waterboarding? Nobody, in my opinion, had the guts to run it and oppose the all-too-powerful Bush.

There is no freedom of publishing in America. Oh, you can print books, well sort of. Some printers will delay a book because of content, and some will outright refuse to print it at all. Sometimes, like in some of my experiences, you will never know who is really behind it. I'm a journalist, so I react against all of this. But I want to make a distinction here. This is not about censorship on issues like child pornography, which does not affect foreign policy, does not affect the public's right to know what its government and elected officials are doing, and does not affect the flow of information about world events. But censoring politically sensitive books, like this one, and others I've published, does. That bothers me immensely, and is what propelled me to write this story.

There is no privacy in America. Every telephone conversation—whether on a cell phone—or on a landline—is monitored and recorded. All the calls are processed through computers and/or satellites through which the government connects the data to its supercomputer system and records everything. As you speak, your conversation is monitored and certain key words and phrases trigger a response team to listen to the recording. There is a priority method and some words like "I'm going to blow up the White House" will initiate extremely rapid attention; others may take hours, or even days for someone to listen to the information. But if those key words come up, someone in law enforcement or intelligence will listen to it eventually.

On cell phones, anyone with a cell phone can be located through the phone. Even if it is turned off, its location can still be determined. Also, any phone numbers stored in a cell phone can be retrieved. How powerful is this tracking? I know of a case where a husband was in a divorce. He was a former police detective who had been trained on how to hack into cell phones and activate the GPS tracking mode so that the police could track suspects. During the divorce and after losing his job with the police department, he used his skills to hack into the cell phone of one of the kids. Whenever his "wife" called that child on her cell phone, he could find out exactly where she was using the GPS tracking system which can be used to track any cell phone.

Of course, anything on a computer can be read if that computer is connected to the Internet. If someone is typing on a computer, any computer, every keystroke generates a signal which can be read from a "smart van" in the neighborhood which can read those signals and tell what you're typing.

Anything being said in a house can be picked up as well.

This type of eavesdropping on American citizens used to require a warrant signed by a judge, and the government agency had to show probable cause and convince a judge that it was justified. Not any more, with the Patriot Act. And what a name for it. As if it is patriotic to blatantly violate the Constitutional rights of all the citizens of this country. President Bush should be ashamed. Every Congressman who voted for the bill should be ashamed. Every American should be ashamed and in an uproar. Every journalist who wrote or said something to support the bill should be ashamed.

And now "terror" includes activism. The *Los Angeles Times* reports that the FBI's highly publicized war against terrorism is being used to gather information on anti-war and environmental protesters! Even activists who feed the homeless are being harassed and investigated. Come on, big brother, just how far down do you have to beat the people to get what you want?

So now, if someone is an antiwar protester, they are defined by the FBI as a terrorist. Isn't that cute. Bush views anyone who protests his war as a terrorist, and therefore subject to surveillance and all the other elements of the Patriotic Act. For a president hell-bent on pouring hundreds of billions of dollars into defense contracting companies and Halliburton, protests in America are a significant threat. Defining protesters as terrorists is absurd, and gives the president such broad powers to control opposition to his administration that Hitler's power to spy on citizens dwarfs in comparison. I commend the *Los Angeles Times* for the article about activism. We need thousands more.

American citizens can now be *spied on* without court review, arrested without any requirement to notify families of the arrest, incarcerated in Guantanamo Bay or anywhere in the world in a black site—*indefinitely*—without the right to see an attorney or appear before a judge, and *tortured*. What could be worse? Bush's prison in Cuba is nothing more than a concentration camp and the thought that an anti-war activist runs the risk of winding up there is horrifying. His prison in Cuba is not any different from Castro's five prisons there. That must give Castro great pleasure to know that Bush has stooped just as low to keep his oil and military-industrial complex stranglehold intact on the United States. How many more secret Bush prisons are there throughout the world? Is it any wonder that so many people throughout the world hate us? Until we address the issue of hatred for America, and how we have contributed to that hatred, we will never win the War on Terror, no matter how many people we spy, arrest, torture, or kill in battles.

Why isn't the media enraged? Is the media afraid they could wind up there themselves? Possibly, but more likely, they're afraid of losing their jobs. I think it's more like the typical US citizen, thinking it can't happen here, it isn't really happening here, this is America, the land of the free, it won't happen to me. Just because they have the power to arrest people and take them away, and people disappear, doesn't mean they'll use that power unjustly, does it? I mean, I'm just a regular citizen. It won't happen to me, will it?

Look at history, people. Look at Hitler. Look at Castro. Look at Iran. Look at what this war in Iraq has cost us in human lives and money—big money—to line the pockets of Bush's partners in defense and oil contracting. Our low gasoline prices were initially part of the excuse for the invasion of Iraq, it was to protect our prices at the pumps, and then *after* the invasion, the invasion became the *reason* for our high prices at the pumps. Bush reminds me of the story of the scorpion who offered the frog a ride on his back. The frog said, "What about your big stinger? You will sting me."

"No I won't," the scorpion promised.

So the frog believed the scorpion, jumped on his back, took the ride, and the scorpion stung him. The frog cried out, "You promised you wouldn't sting me!"

The scorpion said, "But you knew I had the stinger. And it's in my nature."

Ah yes, it was the frog's fault.

And so Nietzsche wrote, "Power corrupts, and absolute power corrupts, absolutely."

When the American public and Congress allow a president to take away all these constitutional rights, we've jumped on the scorpion's back. And we will get stung.

Occasionally we get snippets of news exposing opposition to the extreme abuses of our constitutional rights, but rarely front-page articles, and never on the television. Remember, the television news is not *news*, it is *entertainment*. So if you watch the nightly news on television, you're not informed, and it's not news that you're getting.

In a snippet published in *The Wichita Eagle*, on page 4A, not the front page, the story emerges that five former judges on the nation's most secretive court, including one who resigned in apparent protest over President Bush's warrantless eavesdropping, voiced skepticism at a Senate hearing about the president's constitutional authority to order wiretapping on Americans without a court order. They also, on the same page, reported that the Supreme Court gave a skeptical hearing to the Bush administration's claim that the president has the power to create special military tribunals to try foreigners he deems to be war criminals. Five of the eight justices hearing the case raised issues based on the laws of war and the Geneva Convention, which set basic rules of fairness for trying alleged war criminals. They questioned whether the president was free to ignore those rules. Questioned? Questioned? World courts arrest and try former presidents of other countries for war crimes violating the Geneva Convention, and yet Bush claims he has the right to ignore it? And the media supports it? Questioned? Who has the legal power to stop this? Congress? John Woo advised the President that he didn't have to obey Congress and some of the laws they passed which were directly contrary to what he was doing.

I heard a radio talk-show host discussing the Geneva Convention and the duty for US soldiers to give medical aid to wounded "enemy soldiers" in the field, rather than shoot them in the head and "simply" terminate them. The caller argued that our soldiers had a duty to obey the Geneva Convention, but the talk-show host argued over him asking, "Is beheading allowed in the Geneva Convention?" The caller, now collared, argued that it was impertinent, declaring that we have rules of war and don't want to become the terrorists ourselves. But he was talked over again and his argument faded under the tirade of the host who laughed at him, saying that our soldiers have every right to just shoot a wounded "terrorist" and end it right there. "This is how we have to deal with these people," the host concluded.

That's what Castro concluded shortly after he took power in 1959. He assigned squads to go into Havana and assassinate the intellectuals at the university who opposed him. And he initiated electronic surveillance all over his country, and arrested people at will, no rights, and now Bush is doing it too.

What I am about to write here, apparently and to my knowledge, never got into the news, but when I went to the Miami International Book Fair in 1990, I met with William McCaulley, author of *A Rebel in Cuba* and *The Sandino Affair*. He signed the reprint rights to *A Rebel in Cuba* with me, and we talked as we drove to dinner together that evening. He told me how he had been forced, after Castro took power, to organize and lead the assassination squads to go into Havana and kill all the intellectuals at the university who had opposed Castro. He also told me that the biggest event causing Castro to turn communist was over oil.

"The Soviets had offered to sell him crude oil for pennies compared to what Standard Oil was charging Cuba for crude, and Castro decided to buy the Soviet crude. But Standard Oil, who owned the refinery in Havana, refused to process Soviet crude. Castro insisted that he could buy crude wherever he wanted, and they still refused to process the Soviet crude. So Castro eventually said, 'Okay, gentlemen. It is no longer your refinery,' and he nationalized it. And that marked the end of his business relationship with the United States." You can imagine the affect of that single act on Standard Oil, and the pressure they then put on the US government to break Castro. This is just one story of how importing and exporting oil can have a major affect on US foreign policy and on foreign relations in general. OPEC was formed during the Kennedy Administration and the complexity of oil politics would take new dimensions over the next forty years. There isn't space in this book, or in the whole universe, for that matter, to go into detail on oil politics over the last fifty years, or hundred years. And now, with the invasion of Iraq, oil politics take a whole new dimension, an oil-industrial complex in a partnership with the US Government and military-industrial complex, completely sidestepping and ignoring international law, ignoring the United Nations, and even the Geneva Convention.

On Tuesday, April 4, 2006, Iraqi authorities filed genocide charges against Saddam Hussein, accusing him in a 1980s "crackdown" which killed an estimated 100,000 Kurds in northern Iraq. What they left out was the fact that the first President Bush encouraged the Kurdish uprising, promised air support and a "no fly zone," and promised that Saddam Hussein would not be able to counter the uprising from the air.

The preface to *The White Tribe*, by Robin Moore, a book I published in 1991, described it as a horrifying sight when the Iraqi helicopter gunships swooped down on the fleeing Kurdish rebels. Fixed-wing Iraqi fighter planes backed up the attack, pouring bombs and machinegun fire on rebels and civilians alike. Government tanks, now protected by war planes, finished the job as the rebels fled for the mountains. Bush had promised the rebels that he would keep Saddam's planes on the ground.

Then President Bush reneged on his promise enabling the slaughter, and yet he is not named for any responsibility in the killings. The Kurds have not forgotten this. And we wonder why certain people in that region hate us. It's time to do something about that.

There's something I haven't forgotten, too. It was 1973 and the energy crisis was on. There was such a shortage of gasoline that everyone—coast to coast—was waiting in line for gasoline at the pumps and often the stations simply ran out of gas.

That summer I was twenty-one years old and had just been hired as a chemist in a refinery. As I drove my SS 396 Chevelle from Wichita, Kansas to St. Paul, Minnesota to report for my new job, I was concerned that I might not be able to get enough gas to get to my job to help manufacture gas. I remember waiting in line at the various gas stations on the highways along the way, but I got there. I was also resentful of the price I had to pay. The shortage was the reason for that, too.

I started my job and there were about a hundred or more tests which I occasionally had to perform on crude oil, gasoline, waste water, and various solutions used in the refining process. There were some tests on gasoline which I had to do once and sometimes twice a day. One such test was the Reid Vapor Pressure Test, which measured vapor pressure of gasoline to determine the mix of hydrocarbons in the sample. It's the vapor pressure, or volatility of the gasoline which enables your car to start on a cold morning. It was important to the quality of gasoline which we sold to check this, because in the huge storage tanks (eighty feet tall), the heavy hydrocarbons would settle toward the bottom, and the light hydrocarbons would float to the top.

So we tested the tanks at ten-foot intervals of height, and then we would either re-circulate the bottom gasoline to the top, or perhaps inject propane into the tank to raise the vapor pressure to meet required specs. I remember my first day and the employee who climbed the tanks to take the samples and bring them to me came in, and he was all out of breath. I looked at the sample tray he carried for each tank, and there were eight slots, one for each ten feet of gasoline in the tanks. The sample trays all had seven or eight samples in them.

He said, "I wish they would sell some of this gas. I used to just have to climb twenty or thirty feet. Now they're all full, and I'm having to climb all the way to the top."

I took the samples and the chemist standing next to me said, "I usually only had to test a few from each tank, but now you have to do seven or eight." Basically, it was double the workload for me, but more importantly, *why were all the tanks full when there was a shortage of gasoline?*

I discovered through the next few weeks that not only were all the gasoline storage tanks full, all the crude oil storage tanks were full also. I began to look around and noticed that the semi-trucks bringing in the crude were lined up and waiting to unload, *and had to wait for us to refine some crude oil and make room in the tanks.*

I wasn't a journalist then, but it had a major effect on me. We were also polluting the blazes out of the river nearby, and I knew that first hand also because I tested the various wastewaters which we passed through a lagoon system, supposedly catching all the hydrocarbons we had contaminated the water with. We were also polluting the air with sulfur dioxide.

I decided to quit because it was disgusting—the lies to the American people—about the fake shortage. And the pollution had a factor in it, too. I switched my career to political science, hoping, in the future, to be able to do something about it.

Summarily, it is obvious that the War on Terror is being used to reap huge profits from oil and defense contracting through a military-industrial-oil-government complex. Yes, the partnership has expanded. The oil industry, especially Halliburton, has teamed up with partners like those in The Carlyle Group and defense contracting, and they have joined the government with Bush at the helm to turn hundreds of billions of dollars of tax money into profits for themselves, killing tens of thousands of people along the way, destroying the environment, destroying our freedoms, creating hate for the United States throughout much of the world, and doubling gasoline prices for another huge profit on top of an already gigantic cake. And anyone who actively opposes this is labeled as unpatriotic, and a terrorist.

And look at gasoline prices in America. More than double since Bush took office. Strange result from a president who swore that the war in Iraq was to protect the price of gasoline here in America. When Exxon-Mobil posted record—big record—earnings, there was no shame! Bush had no shame! Gas price is double! Almost triple. It's going up every day. Who allowed the merger between Exxon and Mobil? Like they weren't big enough already. Like we don't need competition in America to keep oil prices down. Americans are being bilked out of billions of dollars over this, and *it's just the beginning unless we get this Patriot Act repealed, stop this senseless war, get a president and Congress who will restore our rights as citizens, and break up this military-industrial-oil-government partnership.*

CHAPTER SIXTEEN
Death by Silence

In the Fall of 2004, I edited and published *The Singleton: Target Cuba* by Robin Moore and Major General (Ret.) Goeffrey C. Lambert.

Lambert commanded the Army Special Forces from 2001 through 2003. He and his Special Forces "Green Berets" conquered Afghanistan. It was brilliant. Lambert trained the men, they learned the language, they grew beards, they went in and converted soldiers, who would have been the enemy, into allies. They recruited soldiers to fight on our side. If the soldiers wouldn't commit allegiance to the Americans, then the Green Berets called in the smart bombs and killed them.

He told me that he only lost seven men to enemy fire. Seven men. He wouldn't tell me how many died from friendly fire, how many got mistakenly hit by the smart bombs they called in against the enemy, that was classified. But to take Afghanistan and only lose seven men to the enemy was phenomenal. For years, the Russians lost tens of thousands of soldiers trying to conquer that country, and they failed.

Working with him, I quickly discovered that Lambert is a brilliant man. While we were editing *The Singleton* we talked a lot about the War in Iraq. He told me that he had disagreed with Bush and Tenet and Rumsfeld as a general but they wouldn't listen to him. He told me he advised them not to go in with big kinetic forces, and especially, that they should not disband the Iraq military.

The military, he explained to me, in a Third-World country, such as Panama (he was there when we took out Noriega) or Iraq, is not just an army to fight for national defense, the army serves numerous functions within the country—they are the police, they are customs, they protect the borders—and if you disband them, you create chaos. Also, you put tens of thousands of men who had a job, retirement, etc., out of a paycheck and on the street, armed, trained, and mad about losing their jobs, especially the officers.

When Bush and Tenet and Rumsfeld disbanded the military in Iraq, they created chaos and cut loose thousands of men who could become terrorists or guerilla fighters against Americans. Also, the invasion of tens of thousands of American troops, not trained in the language and customs, created huge cultural atrocities, not to mention the physical atrocities. The 2003 order by Iraq's then-American governor L. Paul Bremer dismissed 400,000 officers and troops.

Even worse, practically everyone who worked for the government was subsequently fired. Saddam's government and army was run by Sunnis, and now they had all been alienated from the new government which America tried to form. We backed the Shiites, and now (2010) Shiite Prime Minister Nouri al-Maliki and his allies run the present Iraq government support by the USA. Why couldn't they see that they created a religious, internal civil war in Iraq by doing this? We could not then and cannot now possibly win this war in this scenario. Lambert told me he cautioned against this approach, but no one paid heed.

Lambert went to Iraq and led the Green Berets there, securing northern and southern Iraq. In the summer of 2003, General Lambert retired early, and told me it was because of how we invaded Iraq, and that he wanted to write *The Singleton*.

He wrote *The Singleton* as a novel to serve as a blueprint on how the war on terror should be fought, to show that there are alternatives to invading a country the way we did in Iraq, a way to fight the war on terror without killing thousands of people, and having thousands of our own soldiers killed, and blowing everything up.

When we were in the planning stages of the book, I called the printer, and was told I could get ten-day delivery on a trade paperback. So rather than do the hardcover for February or March 2005, we opted to go for the fast softcover to hit the Christmas market of 2004.

The printer did not deliver as promised. Their staff delayed the book, and because of that the books did not hit the chain stores until the day *after* Christmas. So we lost tremendous sales. The general manager was very anti-Bush and perceived this book as pro-Bush, and whatever his reasons, he did nothing to help get this book out on time. His staff seemed to do everything wrong, everything to delay delivery. He'd been my friend for years, but suddenly, over *The Singleton*, he would no longer take or return my phone calls. I've seen this before, it's in earlier chapters, and here it was again.

The Singleton was an "oblique jab" at Bush and Rumsfeld and Tenet for their maladroit invasion of Iraq, according to Ann Scott Tyson, who reviewed the book for the *Christian Science Monitor*. She got it, but it seemed that very few others did. The printer, I'm sure, thought it was pro-Bush and pro-Iraq War.

Christian Science Monitor Book Review
"The age of terror requires smarter, smaller approach"

American intelligence uncovers evidence that Cuba is secretly developing biological weapons in a plan to attack the United States.

Defense Secretary Donald Rumsfeld urges military action to destroy the threat. But President Bush disagrees: "After our experience in Iraq, I don't think the kinetic approach is the answer," he says. "I think the real center of gravity in this issue is Castro's motivation. We must destroy his motivation to continue this program..."

With this oblique jab at the Pentagon's Iraq strategy, veteran Special Forces commander Maj. Gen. (Ret.) Jeff Lambert begins his first novel. "The Singleton: Target Cuba," co-authored with Robin Moore, is a thriller with real-world advice at every turn. In essence, it's a public appeal for a smarter and less costly way for America to defeat foes: using sophisticated 'influence operations' that meld the skills of the CIA, Special Operations Forces, and foreign allies - rather than conventional military force.

Such operations are preferable "in most cases" to avoid "the resultant baggage of invasions and superpower flexing," explains General Lambert. "I am an advocate of using influence operations and surrogate warfare whenever we can unless there is a time-sensitive or overpowering rationale to use our own forces."

Equally vital, he says, the US government must freely tap into expertise across agencies and allies to design the best-qualified team for the mission. "It's a plea for an end to interagency bickering and getting on with the war," he says in an interview, stressing that all have something unique to contribute.

Lambert, who led US Army Special Forces Command during the Afghanistan and Iraq wars, draws on 25 years of experience in the Green Berets that convinced him a handful of highly trained, culturally savvy soldiers - or in this case a "singleton" acting alone - can have far-reaching impact if deftly employed.

Fictional players in "The Singleton" mingle with the real world leaders and events of 2004. The story begins with a blonde British agent in Panama City killing two hit men and saving a Cuban exile, who is delivering documents on Cuba's biological weapons program. A CIA analyst takes the evidence as part of an "agro-terror" plot. Cuba would use migratory birds to deliver an engineered pathogen that would wipe out US wheat crops, causing a severe domestic food shortage as well as a global quarantine and ban on US exports.

In deciding how to respond, President Bush brushes aside Mr. Rumsfeld's proposal for a strike by Tomahawk missiles and ground-penetrating bombs. Instead, he opts for a global, covert operation that CIA director George Tenet promises will convince "Fidel that it is not in his interest to continue."

A CIA-led interagency team known as the "Hybrid" forms to plan a series of disparate intelligence and military operations. It orchestrates an attack on a Sierra Leone diamond mine that helps fund the Cuban program, and sabotages a shipment of German stainless steel tanks. British Prime Minister Tony Blair agrees to let American operatives work under British cover - allowing Washington to deny any involvement.

Yet the most critical and dangerous mission is reserved for (surprise!) a lone Green Beret. The charismatic Maj. Mike Trantor is recovering from wounds to his chest as well as to his marriage from a recent tour in Afghanistan - the latest in a string of deployments that have left his wife, Kirsten, feeling single herself.

Major Trantor's mission: to infiltrate Cuba posing as a British diplomat on a romantic weekend and steal a briefcase from a leading scientist on the program, Mundo Nuevo. What Trantor doesn't know is that a transmitter secretly implanted by a US dentist in one of his teeth is alerting Cuban military forces to his location. In effect, he's being used as bait - to create so much chaos that Cuban leader Fidel Castro will think a foreign-led insurgency is underway and cave in to British pressure to close the program.

Lambert says he wrote the book to impress upon the US public that in the information age, "intelligence is more important than weapons." Meanwhile, technological innovations are offering "unlimited" options for fighting wars.

In reality, such concepts "are all being embraced" within the US government, he says.

The book does not address who would hold accountable the Hybrid as it plans complex, global missions in which disparate organizations coalesce and act in extreme secrecy. Lambert says Congressional oversight would play that role. Lambert also chose not to include a key Green Beret mission - the recuitment, training and mentoring of indigenous forces known as "unconventional warfare"—but says he may in another book.

One weakness of the novel lies in Lambert's fictional treatment of real-life characters such as President Bush in his meetings with cabinet members. Here, the dialogue sounds written not spoken, and some people come across as one-dimensional. Bush, in particular, is unconvincingly flawless.

In contrast, "The Singleton" is at its fast-paced best when Lambert draws on his decades of Special Forces experience to detail Trantor's exhaustive training - from Cuban dialect Spanish to running shoes modified to blend into the barrio - and the high-suspense mission itself.

Ultimately, Lambert's story makes a compelling argument that creative and subtle efforts at persuasion can prove far more effective and less costly in blood and treasure than full-scale military operations.

"Wars are to capture human terrain," he says. "The war on terrorism is a war to change the thinking of billions."

It was a great review, and many who read it seemed to think so too. Ann Tyson is now writing book reviews for the *Washington Post*, and Ron Charles, who was the book review editor for the *Christian Science Monitor*, has also moved to the *Washington Post* as book review editor.

Lambert was very pleased with the review and its content and comments about Bush and Rumsfeld. But when I got him on

Fox News and the *Linda Vester Show*, and the *Jim Bohannon Show*, and NBC's *Crossfire*, he would not speak out and say the things he told me personally, like the fact that Bush had committed so many resources with this mess in Iraq that we had spread our military resources too thin, and were ignoring other problems, such as Chavez and Venezuela.

I begged Lambert to open up to the news and tell the truth, like the six other generals who had come out and openly criticized Bush's war in Iraq. Lambert told me that he now worked in defense contracting, and that if he spoke out, he would lose his job.

Repeatedly, I got Lambert interviews with Greg Jaffe, of *The Wall Street Journal*. They spoke at least seven times over the phone. Jaffe's story could have run on page one, depending on timing, and what Lambert said, and what was happening in the rest of the world—if Lambert would have allowed himself to be interviewed and quoted. One of Jaffe's specific questions was about whether the US was weakening our position in Afghanistan by placing so many troops in Iraq. Lambert refused to comment to him. I argued, telling him that he had a duty to America, and that the American people had a right to know. He still refused.

Then it came out that Able Danger, a secret task force in the Pentagon, was researching cell phone records and conversations to discover terrorists and fight terrorism during the summer just before 9/11. Twice, members of the Able Danger team got the goods on Mohammad Atta, the mastermind of 9/11. Twice, someone in the Pentagon blocked the information from getting delivered to the FBI for action. It now appears that the intelligence existed in the Pentagon to take action against Atta, yet nothing happened. It appears obvious to me that 9/11 could have been prevented.

When this became public, it also became public that huge amounts of data in the computer files of Able Danger were intentionally erased. Ah, the cover up. We know that drill in America, don't we?

Then, it became public that General Lambert had been the Officer in Charge of Able Danger. Once again, he refused to be quoted except to say that he was incensed that the data had been destroyed without his knowledge.

I begged him again to go public with what he knew about Able Danger (which had to be plenty since he was the top officer in the operation) and got him an interview with a writer with the *Washington Post* who was covering the story. Again, he refused, but in this case, I have more understanding and empathy. Maybe he would be violating some top-secret security promise to talk too much about it. That's a shame, because once again, the American public is kept in the dark. And what a dark secret it is, if 9/11 could have been prevented. The intelligence was there.

Ann Scott Tyson reviewing *The Singleton* and getting its message out about the war in Iraq and the War on Terror is not the same as Lambert being quoted on the front-page of *The Wall Street Journal*. What a shame. I didn't sell books and lost my ass financially, Greg Jaffe didn't get the stories he deserved, the *Washington Post* didn't get the stories they deserved, and the American public got screwed out of learning about Lambert's book and how the War on Terror should be fought, and should have been fought in Iraq. Lambert told me he told Bush and Rumsfeld and Tenet not to go into Iraq the way they wanted to, and Lambert said they would not listen to him or the other generals. Several of those other generals have gone public.

Lambert also told me that Iraq was Bush's war, a vendetta.

Before I could put this matter to rest, I had to tell this story and write this chapter. I tried to get the story out in the book, and I tried to get the story out through all the journalists that were willing to interview General Lambert, and who had General Lambert as a guest. I thank and commend all those journalists, especially Ann

Scott Tyson, Ron Charles, Linda Vester, the producers at Fox News, and Jim Bohannon and his producer. Bohannon, interviewing Lambert for his show, very quickly fired a question about a passage in the book concerning Bush and the administration, and asked Lambert if he stood behind the passage in the book. There was a long pause, and then Lambert answered, "No." As far as I was concerned, and probably any one else, that interview was over. I still worked very hard for another year, trying to convince Lambert that he needed to open up, and I got him one final interview with Greg Jaffe. He declined.

In this case, the journalists were willing to give it a go. It was the author who wouldn't deliver. But the issue stopping the flow of information is still—the military-industrial complex—the partnership with government and the military—and General Lambert's paycheck from it.

I think this chapter shows that there were journalists trying their best to get Lambert's story out. They were smart enough to see *The Singleton* in the same light that Ann Scott Tyson did when she wrote about it for the *Christian Science Monitor*. I was very disappointed that the book didn't get any other reviews, but that's the way it goes.

My opinion is that there is a lot of dissatisfaction with Bush and the war in Iraq and that *anything* that even suggests that he's a good president is going to be trashed. Regrettably, Bush did come off too well in *The Singleton*, even though the book is really a slap at him. Few apparently saw it that way, and a vivid example is the way it was received in French translation.

The book was translated into French yet all the major French publishers turned it down. Then, it was pitched to some Moroccan publishers. I got the following email from Morocco:

I received a NO answer from an association of Moroccan publishers – very long and detailed ! –stating that the book is so unduly flattering for Bush that the author and the publisher must have been sponsored by the American government !!!

This is the first time in my career that I've ever had anyone think any of my books were sponsored by the American government. Reading *this* book should easily vindicate me on that one. But I have to take the portrayal of Bush as a valid criticism, and that I do.

CHAPTER SEVENTEEN
Two Different Wars

Suddenly, there is good news on the war in Iraq. On February 27th, 2010 it was announced that 20,000 ousted Iraqi army officers are being reinstated in their jobs. This is the smartest move I've seen by the American government since the war began. I'm glad to be able to report some good news. This is a major step in the right direction, and may produce rays of hope for Iraqis that the religious ousting of Sunnis from the government will continue to be reversed, such that they may after all get their rightful share of government representation.

However, the *Associated Press* report of this action, which I commend, which was wonderful to read, also presented views of skepticism about this move and quoted critics who said the move was linked to the election and gaining votes. So what? The fact is that it can contribute significantly to persuading the insurgency that their best strategy is to join the new government rather than try to blow it up and kill Americans. Now that the doors appear to be opening, they can now participate in the new government and vote! Isn't that what we're supposed to be doing there—setting up a democracy for all Iraqis to participate in their own government and vote? Come on, American media, get on the stick!

In this chapter of the book, I bring forward aspects of the wars in Iraq and Afghanistan which I feel the news has either not covered at all or has only briefly reported. So I bring it forward here for

America to read to get some information based on first hand reports from people who have been there and shared this information with me. This enables me to present a perspective here which I feel is very relevant to how our country moves forward in these wars.

What the news in general sometimes touches on, but never exactly seems to cover, is that the war in Afghanistan and the war in Iraq are quite different. They were, in effect publically treated the same. Consider the following information in this light.

Regarding Iraq, the West must shoulder significant blame for the problems post-Sadaam and the slow transition to an Iraqi government.

First, the US representative there, L. Paul Bremer, fired everyone in the government or military of any significant rank because they were from Sadaam's Bath party. What the West failed to understand (as Patton did in WWII rebuilding German and allowing "former Nazis" to participate) is that such an action gutted the country of anyone with any experience. When you live under a dictator like Sadaam and he says "join my party or die," many joined to stay alive.

Second, there is also the fact that the majority of the Iraqi population bears some responsibility for events there. When one of my sources was in Iraq a few years ago, he led a portion of a study for the USG on the Iraqi Army. As part of that, he spent a lot of time with various commanders and units of the Iraqi Army. One such event was several days with an Iraqi commander responsible for guarding large sections of Iraq's oil pipeline. They were sitting in his office one night and a news clip came on of people being interviewed on TV. The reporter was interviewing people in the street after a car bomb and lamenting with them how bad the Americans were for allowing it to happen, and how bad the Iraqi military was for not preventing it and not keeping them safe. Someone asked him what he thought of it. His reaction was succinct and blunt.

He told the people in the room he was sick of how Westernized the media in his country had become and he was embarrassed about his countrymen who'd become "sheep." With growing emotion in his voice and the fire in his eyes gaining in intensity, he said, "Look. I was one of Sadaam's tank battalion commanders in the Iran - Iraq war. In one day we lost almost 10,000 soldiers. By the next morning I had 10,000 more. That day he made us attack again. We lost almost 9,000 soldiers. It went on and on." He continued: "In the first gulf war I was a brigade commander. We lost thousands in every American attack. He sent more. Same in this war. I was glad to see the Americans come. It stopped the slaughter. Now I see my countrymen on TV complaining when 5, 10, 15 people are killed by an insurgent bomb. What are they doing to fight back? Nothing. They know where these people live. They are so accustomed to being cared for like sheep, and they expect everyone to take care of them when they know who and where these people are. And many in the press—they sensationalize this when they should be leading the world opinion against the atrocities."

Third, there is the blame the West in general must bear. Everyone criticized this Iraqi brigade commander and his troops for letting insurgents damage the pipeline and interrupt the flow of oil. When you looked at it "on the ground," you had a pipeline guarded by Pipeline "Security Battalions" by putting 1-2 guys out in the middle of nowhere with three rounds of ammunition, living under a tarp, and literally, with no shoes. Some were lucky if they even had a blanket. Most had not been paid in MONTHS. And we blamed them for running when insurgents came up heavily armed, and it was them or a length of pipe?

In another finding, there is much criticism by the west (fueled by more than a few journalists) that Iraqi Security Forces and some critical Iraqi emergency response services are not training to capacity (schools, units) or operating at sufficient levels to be self-sufficient.

After the end of hostilities, coalition forces stopped fuel issued to the Iraqi Army, in part, to force them to be independent. The rations of fuel from the Government of Iraq were inadequate to meet the training and some joint ISF/CF operational needs. The real problem was that the available fuel supply in Iraq (diesel and benzene) were inadequate to support even the national demand regardless of Iraqi Security Forces (ISF) needs. What seemed to escape the press was the simple fact that Iraq does not produce sufficient quantities of fuel to support even minimum national requirements to include ISF. As one oil industry expert, charged with re-building the Iraqi oil infrastructure, put it: "Iraq's oil system was built completely opposite of any other oil producing country in the world. It was designed simply to make Saddam money."

Iraq must buy a majority of the benzene and diesel it consumes. Iraq's oil infrastructure was built to export crude oil. Until recently, there was only one operating refinery. Octane level of benzene produced was too low to be useable, requiring fuel to be shipped to Turkey for additives, and then re-imported. This situation will continue for at least the next 3-5 years.

Stability in Iraq also suffered because of an unresponsive ISF pay and personnel system, contributing to high rates of soldiers and Non-Commissioned Officers (NCOs) leaving the ISF due to failure of the government of Iraq to pay and promote them. ISF soldiers, NCOs and officers are not being paid in a timely manner; they must travel back to their old units after transfer to be paid; or, soldiers are being paid at a lower rank. Soldiers' correct status, rank, or unit were not being reflected on the ISF pay rosters or in pay issued. Changes to soldier unit of assignment are not being made to the ISF personnel system; and changes to soldier promotions are not being reflected in the ISF personnel system. Personnel transactions affecting pay take an average of 6 12 months to be approved at the MOD and go into effect once submitted.

Implementation of the Anti-Corruption initiative resulted in an aversion at the ministerial level to approving any transactions for fear of corruption allegations and the associated incarceration until the accusation is investigated. Multiple signatures are an effective means to avoid a corruption allegation. As a result, some seventeen signatures are required to approve a single pay transaction—up to fifteen signatures just to get approval to promote a soldier. No process is currently in place to expeditiously deal with the administrative burden or the backlog generated from rebuilding the ISF and Ministries after being disbanded by the Coalition Provisional Authority (CPA).

Finally, remember the big scandal of those guys caught "stealing oil" from Iraq and trying to smuggle it over the border to sell it? Ever wonder why you never heard what happened to them? That's because they were set free. Why? Because they weren't really stealing oil. This intrigued one of my sources so much that he literally found the one guy in Iraq responsible for re-building the Iraqi oil infrastructure. The truth is that there was so much good publicity in touting another corruption story on Iraq that no one bothered to cover the fact that stolen crude oil is virtually useless. You can't burn it, and without knowing its source and quality, most refineries won't buy it—especially just one truckload. That particular shipment wasn't oil at all. It was waste oil by-product from the refinery in Iraq—and legal to export. But that didn't fit the story line.

The moral of the story is not that the media is bad, just that, as much as there are all the bad things going on which get written about regarding the government side, there are some in the media that contribute to the deteriorating situation.

Earlier in the book, I express my opinion that the War in Iraq was launched illegally. It was reported that then-President Bush (and Cheney) knew that there were no Weapons of Mass Destruction in Iraq, and invaded anyway.

Again, Afghanistan is a different story. The problem in Afghanistan is that we started with a campaign that supported the local army (which we didn't have in Iraq) and Afghanis took back Afghanistan for Afghanis. At that point, we turned it into a conventional fight like Iraq and relegated them to a subordinate role.

In Afghanistan, as in most crisis areas, stability of the country depends on the relationship and balance of seven capital forms— Political, Natural, Economic, Infrastructure, Cultural, Social, and Human. The actions in Iraq critically degraded the political, cultural, and social capital of the people and the leaders. In Afghanistan, when the focus shifted to destroying the Taliban, and the Northern Alliance that essentially won the war was pushed into the shadow by a huge multi-national force "rebuilding the country" run by outsiders, the Karzai government lost political capital with the people. Economic capital fell with the inability of the local population to sustain itself with a meaningful label. They became dependant on outside aid and outside armies for protection. Human capital and the social capital holding it all together diminished as well.

The recent strategy you see being put in place by General McChrystal is a return to focus on the Afghanistan people and rebuilding many of these capital forms. Unfortunately, as is our practice in the West, our president has essentially said, "Look. We came in and wrecked your country. We're going to throw 30,000 more troops in there to stabilize it, but we're pulling out next summer before the elections here. So you better come up to speed fast."

Colonel Robert Morris has a comment on this last. "When I see stuff like that I remember a session I had at the Army Command and General Staff College when a dear friend of mine, the first post-genocide Rwandan Ambassador to the United States, spoke there. The Ambassador lost his father in the first Rwanda Genocide back in the 1960s. His father had been crucified. In the intervening years he lived with his family as a refugee all over central Africa going from refugee camp to refugee camp, wherever his mother could get them an education. One time it was so bad his mother actually took them all to the river with the plan to drown them all, and herself. She didn't. He became the first post-genocide Rwandan Ambassador to the US and then Chief of Staff to the President there. After one of the most eloquent presentations I've heard on Rwanda, a young officer, in an obvious attempt to make a name for himself among his peers, piped up during question-and-answer time to ask: "'So, I understand about the genocide and all, but how long is it going to be before there is total equality for Hutus and Tutsi's in Rwanda under your new government?'

"The Ambassador's answer was as profound as it was gentle and simple: 'I think when you look at the scope of the challenge we face in reaching such equality in Rwanda and considering just emerged from genocide as a nation and so must now repatriate over 1 million refugees, the best comparison I can offer is to ask you how long it took for blacks and women in America to achieve complete and total equality and freedom from bias.'"

This book is a call to writers, journalists, producers, and news entities to bring forth in-depth news and "eye on" news which gets to the heart of the situations in Iraq and Afghanistan, and deliver information which can help an informed public decide issues for themselves, and ultimately, who to vote for.

CHAPTER EIGHTEEN
Corporatism and Millions of Minions

The Supreme Court just ruled in *Citizens United v. Federal Election Commission* that corporations have the same right as citizens to spend money and produce media with respect to political issues, campaigns, politicians, or any other political purpose. From the first day that corporations were granted the right by the US government to form and engage in activities in commerce, they have been barred from such activity and spending. Unless their business was directly the business of information or news, there were severe criminal penalties for violating the laws which were wisely written to protect the people of this nation from corporate power and to ensure that the government is "by the people, for the people."

Now the bar has been removed in a gesture seemingly as simple as the brush of a fly off of a table. The impact upon society and government, however, could turn out to be the biggest blow to democracy that this nation has ever faced. It could turn out to prove some of the science fiction writers correct: the end of the nation-state.

This single ruling could enable corporations, once and for all, to bark orders to candidates and politicians, and when they disobey there can be so much bite that it goes beyond my imagination as a writer and publisher. It is easy to imagine a massive, expensive smear campaign in the media, the cost of which to a corporation such as a major drug manufacturer could be miniscule in comparison to the revenue they may be able to receive in the market if they get government to do what they want. Beyond even my imagination is the effect on society of such massive media power and how it could be used by corporations. Think about defense contracts, or the ability to remove regulations and trade laws. Think about the publishing of books.

All publishers rely on news giants for publicity—CBS, NBC, ABC, *Fox News*, radio, *The Wall Street Journal* and major newspapers and magazines—mostly owned by major corporations. It is a fairly widely held belief that the content is corporate driven, not only through commercials directly, but by what the sponsors want to see in the programming in general.

The business of books is content driven, and unless our house is owned by a major corporation, they have little or no control over what we publish. However, because of the extent of their control over major media and before this ruling, the corporations had more than enough power to affect the success of a book. Now that power seems even more threatening. Now our content has to compete with their content, in addition to competing for time on the air or space in print. The fact that the CBS special glorifying corporatism and CEOs in America directly follows the Super Bowl in programming is a metaphor for what's to come. Sometimes a book publisher (not one owned by Newscorp) hopes to see a special on their book or author, or someone who has contributed to humanity. To quote Hemingway, "Wouldn't it be pretty to think so."

President Obama seems entirely free to joke about owning GM. But soon, I suspect this partnership between government and big business will shift, and one day some CEO will respond to some question about the government and say, "I own it." Big Brother, which today I see as that partnership, seems likely to become the corporations themselves.

I find it insulting for Americans to see Oprah Winfrey and CBS patting CEOs and their corporations on the back. I do not feel the same compassion for the CEOs and the huge corporations in America, some of whom have recently been bailed out with huge sums of money from the government. My compassion goes to the millions of minions, or what's left of them, who serve those corporations and live in poverty, or have miserable lives, or live on antidepressants just to do their job, and who will be forced to live in a country where Big Brother will not only be listening, but speaking.

Summarily, it is apparent that Putin is building his own oil-industrial complex, a partnership between a "shadow" energy oligarchy and the Kremlin. And he is not going to let Bush's American-based oil-industrial complex get control over Yukos. This was apparent by his arrest of Yukos' top executive Mikhail Khodorkvsky and his block of the sale of 25 percent of Yukos stock to Exxon Mobil. This was a clever move. Putin basically nationalized Yukos after foreign investors built the company up with foreign capital. Some of the American investors are fighting back with a lawsuit.

Not once in the national news in the US have I seen the word nationalized used to refer to Yukos. How would Americans react if they knew that the privatization process had been used to gain foreign investment and now a re-nationalizing process was being used to retain control of the energy companies by an oligarchy partnership with the Kremlin. We're only seeing the beginning. Think back to Peter Grinenko's testimony before Senator Ben Knighthorse Campbell and the Commission.

Corporate leaders and business people who don't agree with the Kremlin find themselves in deep trouble. Putin obviously has the same kind of power that Bush had, to eavesdrop on citizens and arrest them or harass them. And he, like Bush, is using this power to protect the new oil and gas elite. American Bill Browder is an example. He is banned from entering the country. He and other corporate leaders who didn't agree with the Kremlin wound up in deep trouble. Browder is excluded from entering Russia on the grounds that he is a national security threat.

Some international news articles reveal that the new oil and gas dynasties are visible on practically every corner of Moscow. They are the new rich. They flaunt their new wealth wearing all sorts of brand-name products. They no longer want foreigners in their clubs. As for the Russian companies that created all of this wealth, they no longer need overseas investment.

I recall a long-ago conversation with Peter Grinenko—a discussion about the privatization of Russian businesses and the opportunities for Americans to invest in Russian stock—and he laughed raucously. He told me that Russians look at money invested in stock as free money. Good luck trying to get anything back.

When certain Kremlin opponents during Putin's presidency tried to gather for a G8 summit to discuss the handling of foreign investments and investors, they couldn't even complete the journey to make it there. Some were arrested, removed from trains, or beaten. Putin declared, well ahead of the G8 summit, that some international partners were using the issue of democracy to try to influence Russian internal affairs. He accused the west of focusing on "neocolonialism" which he referred to as a remnant of cold war thinking.

Dick Cheney, the US vice-president at the time, had recently criticized Russia's record on democracy. Maybe he was simply expressing sour grapes over oil deals gone south. In my opinion, Cheney and Bush had been cleverly outmaneuvered by a wily fox. Putin described Cheney's remarks as an "unsuccessful hunting shot," referring to Cheney's hunting accident where he shot a companion with a shotgun.

Chapter Next
A New Decade

Now, in 2010, Baker & Taylor is under new ownership. The Carlyle Group sold the company several years ago to an accounting firm in Chicago. The company, under the new ownership, does not seem to be engaging in any of the negative practices which have occurred in the past, and in my opinion Baker & Taylor is very open to carrying books published by small presses. I recommend Baker & Taylor as a wholesaler.

Barnes and Noble now searches equally the Ingram and Baker & Taylor databases for a book. In addition it appears that their clerks search up to seventeen wholesalers to find books for customers. The Ingram lock has been broken, at least that one.

Steve Riggio, the current CEO of Barnes and Noble appears to be taking the company in directions which are very positive for authors and small presses. His efforts are to be commended. According to a *Publishers Weekly* article on January 24th, 2010 (the day I write this), written by, ironically, Jim Milliot, "Barnes and Noble to Become E-Commerce Retailer." Riggio says company e-book sales have "simply exploded." He also said that for some titles, their market share of e-books is higher than its share for printed books, and that the company is committed to delivering digital content any way the customer wants it, across a variety of devices ranging from the iPhone to Blackberrys.

This is good news for authors and publishers. This is good news for America where books are, in my opinion, increasingly important for citizens to get real information about our country and the world in an age where the news media has demonstrated its limitations.

If you get to read this last paragraph, then you've probably already found this book. It is available wholesale through Bookazine, a wholesaler in New Jersey. I recommend these people also. Perhaps they too, can grow to join the major wholesalers and achieve major availability for the titles they carry. Maybe you didn't find this book in a traditional bookstore or chain store. Maybe you bought it on the Internet. As you now know, an author and publisher can only do what they can do in the midst of American corporatism.

Also there are widespread accounts of people declaring that 80 percent (or more) of the books now sold in bookstores are self-published. If it's not true now, it probably soon will be. Also, that most of the major houses are losing money and facing financial woes. The Internet has blown the market for self-published books and self-distribution wide open. It appears that Americans are developing their own voices and shouting out to the world via their own books. This movement may be enough to shock the media back to reality and into raising and covering new issues. The hope is that the media will center on the best of these books for news stories. But my optimism is tempered by the entire body of the text of this book: that the media is corporate-dollar driven, that the corporations now have more power than ever, thanks to a few presidents and the Supreme Court, and that the books published by their sister companies—and especially those which glorify the huge corporations and their CEOs—will be the ones publicized in the news.

If so, so be it. I've fought this for at least fifteen years. Maybe it's time for Americans to look for books to get the real news, browse the Internet, and read.

INDEX